I0606383

#

Beauty, Neuroscience & Architecture

Published by Fibonacci, LLC

Denver, Colorado

Sept. 1, 2017

Second Printing February, 2022

Distributor: University of Oklahoma Press

Inquiries should be addressed to Donald H. Ruggles, 450 East 17th Avenue, PH 2, Denver, Colorado 80203.

ISBN 978-0-692-92862-2

Printed in the United States of America

Book design by John Boak | boakart.com

I believe in the redemptive power of beauty.

Beauty is not romantic. Beauty is profound.

Beauty is one of the most important emotions in life.

Beauty can save the world, one person at a time.
I am sure of that.

RENZO PIANO, ARCHITECT, CHARLIE ROSE INTERVIEW, SPRING, 2017

Beauty, Neuroscience & Architecture

Timeless Patterns and Their Impact on Our Well-Being

Donald H. Ruggles, AIA

To my parents Don and Madelyn, who inspired a life filled with beauty.

To my wife Nancy, whose daily love is the very essence of beauty.

To my children Chloe and Derek: I am sure I learned more about beauty from you than I ever taught to you.

To my late sister Elaine, whose always-beautiful spirit lives on.

CONTENTS

FOREWORD

Color, texture, pattern, form, scale — these are ordinary words that connect us to what we see.

When we observe great art or architecture, fashion or nature, we use descriptors to identify what we have seen. Perhaps the painting, building or dress is bland, uninspiring, boring — or beautiful, rich, ornate.

We deploy visual cues to penetrate our thought process. The onion-shaped, richly colored domes of St. Basil's Cathedral in Moscow read as fanciful, shapely, specific, while the twin towers and ornate facade of Notre Dame read as strong and magnificent in their design and extraordinary craftsmanship. On the other hand, the Disney Concert Hall in Los Angeles inspires a new train of thought with intersecting bends and new materials.

When taking in such experiences, I use my sensory fields to help me decide how I feel and think about what is in front of me based on what I like and what is familiar. This is a simplistic approach.

But Don Ruggles is reaching deeper and looking for an entirely original perspective. He is a friend, fellow classicist and a thoughtful humanistic architect whose intellectual approach to houses and spaces always gives his clients more than they could have imagined.

Don has carved out personal contemplative time to analyze his clients' reactions to the spaces he has created for them. Of course, they say the house is beautiful; the process of designing and building is collaborative, and there should be no surprises at the end. But their reactions are more than emotional. Don was curious to know what triggered the response, and his exploration led him to an unexpected place — science.

Throughout his journey, Don has asked new questions and searched for a unique methodology to study the interwoven impact of architecture on our brains, biology and well-being. In the process of this thoughtful exploration, he has birthed a new word, "neuro-architectology." His original theories, research and clear thought process make Don a leader of our design community. Don is leading a universe that engages all of our senses and biology. The quest not only deepens the scholar's appreciation for the subject matter, but also draws in those who are just beginning to see and question what makes great art and architecture.

— Barbara Sallick, July 2017

ACKNOWLEDGMENTS

First, let me acknowledge the contribution of my parents Don and Madelyn, who provided continual teaching, guidance, inspiration and love that led directly to this work.

My wife Nancy has been the loving presence in my life for decades now and that loving support led directly to this book. Her endless editorial support and encouragement is without compare. It is impossible to comprehend how this book would exist without her dedication to it.

My children, Chloe and Derek, have been incredible supporters of this effort and given me continual loving encouragement. My son-in-law Carl Vine has been an important supporter too, providing encouragement, editorial support and brilliant insights that have affected the direction I have taken in the writing. Importantly, it was Carl who initially conceptualized the term "neuro-architectology," which started a new line of thought.

Finally, my sister Diane and her husband John McCormack, my stepfather Earl Conley and my brother Randall have provided endless support and encouragement. I am deeply indebted to all of you for so strongly supporting this work.

John Boak of BoakArt in Denver designed the book. John has been a longtime collaborator with our firm, and I am so grateful to have his brilliant talent and thinking woven into this book. The beautiful graphics are his work and are a significant part of the message embodied in the book. A sincere expression of gratitude goes to John.

The editorial quality of the book is the result of Bruce Goldberg, of BG Writes, working as the official editor of this endeavor. His guidance and leadership somehow have managed to keep us all focused on the task while at the same time respecting the fundamental message. It has been a masterful effort on his part.

I also owe so much to my longtime business partner, Melissa Mabe-Sabanosh. Melissa's enthusiasm, intelligence and unwavering commitment to beauty is and has been a constant source of inspiration. Her collaboration on this project has been fundamental to its success.

I am also deeply indebted to Dakota Walters from our firm, who has dedicated hundreds of hours to this effort. She has been an exceptional assistant for two years, lending her critical eye and insightful guidance to the research and editorial quality of this book as well as creating many of the drawings. I owe so much to her dedication to this.

Chuck Rankin of the Oklahoma University Press has been absolutely amazing the entire time, beginning with the first meeting almost two years ago. His support and guidance gave me the confidence that this book and this message was worth writing about. I am deeply indebted to Chuck for all of his kindness and thoughtful leadership, and the time he committed to help move this along.

Also, there are four associates that I must mention.

Barbara Sallick has penned the Foreword and I am so grateful for that. A lecture that Barbara and I gave in 2010 on "Timeless Design" started me on this journey. Barbara is the founder of Waterworks, and the beautiful products it makes helped to inspire me to write this work.

LANTERN IN A SMALL SHINTO SHRINE, TOKYO, JAPAN

Meredith Banasiak has provided critical encouragement from a scholastic and neuroscience perspective, and I am grateful for her editorial comments and guidance confirming much of the science presented here.

Elizabeth Jumel of Jumel Public Relations has been an important part of our team for many years. Her leadership, quiet confidence and expertise helped us to develop these beautiful ideas. Her ability to see beyond the obvious and to frame the larger picture never fails to inspire.

Victor Arango, Studio Candela, brought a worldly view and marketing expertise to the team, and provided important insights, leadership and vision.

I would like to extend my sincere thanks to all the members of my staff. Your continued support and kind words have been so helpful.

Finally, a thank you to my many amazing clients over the years who have provided me and our firm, Ruggles Mabe Studio Architecture & Interior Design, with the opportunities to work on beautiful projects. I am grateful to each and every one of you.

OPPOSITE: MIRADOR DE LINDARAJA IN THE PALACIO DE LOS LEONES, ALHAMBRA PALACE COMPLEX, GRANADA, ANDALUSIA, SPAIN

Special thank yous go to my clients and friends Bruce and Martha Clinton, who provided important editorial reviews of the early manuscripts, and to Judi and Robert Newman, who continue to support beauty in our community in so many ways.

This has been a great team effort that I have had the privilege to lead. I am deeply indebted to all those listed above.

THE PROPOSED MILE-HIGH ILLINOIS
FRANK LLOYD WRIGHT, 1957

PREFACE

Curious. How could beauty, such a personal and subjective emotion, possibly be connected with neuroscience, one of the most intellectual and objective branches of medicine? That is a good question. And how could they possibly be linked to art and architecture, and to our sense of well-being? It turns out they are strongly linked and the linkage affects our daily lives. It has been such for thousands of years.

Beauty, Neuroscience & Architecture attempts to overlay concepts from neuroscience with art and architecture, and illustrate how architecture affects our brains, biology and well-being. As we have come to understand more about how our biology and our minds work, there are great lessons to be learned by those in art and architecture. I intend to illuminate some of these concepts in the chapters ahead, and to propose a path forward to help architects and designers create ways to cut stress and improve people's health while also building a more beautiful world. Along the way, I will share some stories from the 60-year journey that has brought me and our firm, Ruggles Mabe Studio Architecture and Interior Design, to this point.

Interestingly, it all started so innocently. I was watching an interview take place on a small black-and-white television, the family's proud new purchase. It was 1957 and I was 7 years old. I had no idea at the time, but the interviewer was Edward R. Murrow. The older gentleman being interviewed captivated me. I could not take my eyes off him. There was something unusual in his demeanor. He had a presence.

As they talked, a picture flashed across the small silver screen and my life changed forever. I was awestruck. A door burst open in my mind and the future flew in. The gentleman was Frank Lloyd Wright, and the picture was of a proposed building one mile tall, called The Illinois. It was beautiful. I was inspired.

Today, as I look at my profession, I am struck by how architectural education has rendered the words "beauty" and "inspiration" irrelevant. They have become tattered, romantic notions from a forgotten time. This is a grave misstep. Beauty and inspiration have a fundamental role to play in our lives and our well-being. More importantly, thanks to recent advances in neuroscience, biology and psychology, we can prove it. This is an incredibly exciting development for humankind.

In recent years, I have come to reflect upon a lifelong relationship with architecture that started on that day in 1957. As my mind replays the thousands of hours of hard work, designing and building, it is now obvious to me that beauty and inspiration have been common, enduring threads along the way from the beginning.

I wrote this book out of a love for the profession of architecture and the arts. It is written for the nonprofessional reader as well as for the professional, and is intended to be enlightening and inspirational. The writing takes an interdisciplinary approach to the subject matter, drawing upon philosophy, history, psychology, biology, architectural theory, neuro-aesthetics and neuroscience. I call it neuro-architectology. By incorporating the accumulated knowledge of these disciplines, the designer and architect will have a broader understanding of the consequences of their decisions. In sum, we can strive to improve the well-being of societies and individuals worldwide by implementing a new approach to how we think about architecture and design.

In the early 20th century both the Bauhaus and Le Corbusier foretold a "new dawn" for man that envisioned a new order. The sun now has risen on the dawn and is shining brightly on a new age for man. The advent of the neuro revolution is unlocking secrets that portend enriching and ennobling beauty at every turn.

DONALD H. RUGGLES, ARCHITECT

RUGGLES MABE STUDIO

DENVER, COLORADO

2017

43

INTRODUCTION

AWAKENING

We stood in the cathedral-like space, admiring the bright silver streak of a brilliant Colorado sun. It warmed the massive stone column that stood proud in the center of the room. The majesty of the Rocky Mountains surrounded us, separated only by the towering sheets of glass that gave a southerly view. The energy of this single shaft of sunlight brought hope and energy to the room. It was ancient, comforting and nourishing.

"It's beautiful" boomed a voice entering the room. A friend of the owners had just walked in for her first visit. We were in Aspen. It was 1972.

It's "beautiful." What did that mean? I had just dedicated three years of my life to designing this home, my first big project. I used every architectural concept I knew: rhythmic proportions, grids, repetitive math, bold massing, interlocking planes, cantilevered forms and unique textures. No effort had been spared to blend every element of the architectural theories of the time. And the comment was, "It's beautiful."

I hadn't the slightest idea what that word meant. Judging from the tone of voice and the look on the visitor's face, though, it was a good thing. It felt positive and reinforcing. I was left to ponder that brief interaction as the discussion quickly moved to skiing and other events of the day.

I was emboldened with confidence from the seeming success of this first project and soon started work on a second residence in Denver. The site was simply breathtaking, and the program was bold. It took two years to build the home. The owners were having a celebratory party. Having used the same rigorous ideas in this home that were so influential in the first home, I was full of anticipation about more "beautiful" comments.

Frankly, I was not prepared for what happened. They described it instead as "exciting," "interesting" and "unique." And there were a lot of questions about, "Why did you do this or that?" The reaction and the mood were clearly different from the first home, with not one comment regarding beauty. And just like the first home, I had no idea at all why the reactions were what they

FIG 0.1

THE VILLA BORGHESE, ROME

were. Somehow the impacts of each home were diametrically opposed. It was something to think about.

Soon thereafter, with a few more projects completed, I moved to Paris to experience the European lifestyle and to take the grand tour of architectural sites. Having been duly indoctrinated in the Bauhaus vocabulary of the day, the works of Le Corbusier, Mies van der Rohe, Walter Gropius, Eero Saarinen, Alvar Aalto and James Sterling made up my list of sites to visit. These were the touchstones, the benchmarks to which all were compared.

What was more important than viewing, experiencing and absorbing these new ideas? I spent many days at the Fondation Le Corbusier, reviewing his archives. It was an exciting and novel period of discovery for me.

After months of venturing high and low, experiencing these genius modern architects and their profound works, I began to sense that something was missing. It was a feeling that the experience was incomplete and unfulfilling, as if the final note in the symphony hadn't yet been struck. Could these great works, which had been so admired, be missing something?

FIG 0.2
THE VILLA BORGHESE, ROME

Museums had been part of life since my youth. My parents frequently took the family on museum trips. Natural history, art, science, you name it. If there was a museum close by, chances were we were going. Sure to form, prior to leaving for Europe, I got a much-anticipated reminder from my parents, "Don't forget to take time to visit the museums. The Prado, Louvre, Tate, Uffizi; you'll find your own too."

While my primary focus was viewing the great, post-World War II modern works, my parents' words kept ringing in the back of my head and, dutifully, I made sure to throw in the occasional stop at a museum. Frankly, I found these excursions quite nourishing and uplifting. The timeless quality of the sites combined with the exquisite craft of the architecture and genius artistic works all added up to a series of beautiful experiences.

Then, late one afternoon, exhausted and on yet another tour of a historic museum home, I took a seat. There was nothing modern to be seen here. I was in the Villa Borghese in Rome. It was 1974. I was resting quietly on a bench, admiring the window in front of me and entirely lost in the moment. The window had such wondrous detail and scale.

Despite being hundreds of years old, there was something familiar in its proportions. I experienced a sense of connection. As I gazed out at Rome through the window, a great wave of imagination washed over me. I suddenly realized what was missing from the contemporary works that I had been viewing so earnestly: They lacked an emotional component. Rational and functionalist to a fault, the epic works of the modern movement were distilled ones that had left behind a very important component.

To me, Rome was "beautiful." The Villa Borghese was "beautiful." I didn't know what this meant. It was a feeling, and one that had been evoked intuitively. While a few of the modern works I'd been studying and touring were emotionally moving, for the most part, they lacked this other component — beauty.

As I looked upon Rome that day, the view in front of me encapsulated ideas developed over thousands of years. At the root of them was something intuitively more important to architecture than I experienced in many of the contemporary works I was touring. My mind raced back to the comment about my first home in Aspen: "It's beautiful."

FIG 0.3
THE VILLA SAVOYE
LE CORBUSIER

I was never inclined toward subjective debate about what is or what is not beautiful. It is normal and healthy that everyone has their own opinion. But what came to me in front of that window in the Villa Borghese was the notion that perhaps there are some universal components to architecture, some elements in design that create a physical and intuitive connection that is beneficial and life-affirming. The more I looked, the more I sensed the wisdom of these elements in architecture. These were perhaps lessons that had been learned before. In that moment, these thoughts formed a direction that would shape my career for decades to come.

Thus began a lifelong quest to understand beauty. For the longest time, I did not know what it meant. I just knew it was real and that it was important. Thankfully, it kept showing up in assessments of our work. Time after time, new clients would call and say, "Your work is beautiful. Would you like to work with us?" I had very little understanding of what they were referring to, but the prospect of a new project was always encouraging.

So this work is the result of the quest to understand some of the universal fundamentals of beauty as applied to art and architecture. It has been, and very much remains, a fascinating journey. After all, we're just getting warmed up!

GVSTAV
KLIMT.
19 07

1 | BEAUTY

LOOKING FOR INSIGHTS

Those who contemplate the beauty of the earth find reserves of strength that will endure as long as life lasts.
RACHEL CARSON, *SILENT SPRING*

Have you ever been in a room that you didn't want to leave? Was it a space that calmed you, made you feel whole, nourished, hopeful? Have you known a building or a piece of art that you went out of your way to engage with on a routine basis?

Or conversely, have you experienced a room that is unsettling, one that overwhelms the senses to the point of discomfort? Did you sense you had to leave as quickly as possible?

A more general question is, are we subconsciously aware of buildings that we routinely approach or avoid? This is the power of architecture and design at work, and neuroscience is unlocking the ideas of art and architecture that have such an effect on us, whether positive or negative, and why they do.

In roughly 400 B.C., Plato wrote that the three ultimate values were truth, goodness and beauty. Vitruvius wrote in the first century B.C. that the three fundamental components to architecture were strength, utility and beauty. Then in the 16th century, Andrea Palladio wrote that the three essentials were firmness, commodity and delight. All were masters that worked hundreds of years apart, agreeing that there are three basic qualities of a successful building: structure (form), program (use) and aesthetics (beauty).

For over 2,500 years, man has been on an introspective journey to understand beauty: how it applies to our lives, how it affects us and how to create it. That journey was in earnest until roughly the early 1900s, when the modern movement theorized that form, utility and craft should be the new trilogy, and that beauty was no longer the goal of architecture and art.

The Bauhaus, the German art school that operated from 1919 to 1933, led the modern movement. Walter Gropius was its founder. This craft school established that a more utilitarian style of design should lead the way. It was a school whose ideology was the result of developments that evolved from the Industrial Revolution in the 1800s as well as the rebuilding effort of Europe following World War I. Massive construction efforts were needed immediately, which caused time and finance to become dominant factors during this process.

There were new technologies that developed during this era that had a dynamic effect on design. These were plate glass, steel and elevators, as vertical transportation systems, reinforced concrete, central heating and air-conditioning systems, and internal plumbing. These technologies established an invigorating new vocabulary for architecture and offered the hope of a future that re-evaluated old values and established a new model for life.

FIG. 1.1
MONA LISA
LEONARDO DA VINCI

FIG. 1.2 FACING
BASILICA OF ST. PETER, ROME
DONATO BRAMANTE

As the European movement gained a foothold in architecture and art, so followed the United States in adopting this new movement as the singular intelligent approach to the baby boom expansion and the industrial maturation of the Free World. It was perceived as the only path forward, and our educational institutions — led by Harvard University, Yale University and the Illinois Institute of Technology — started teaching the new theories. It was a massive reset for the art and architectural worlds that still holds to this day. The new model was focused on economy and function, and beauty was set aside. Yet the human need for beauty persisted and we continued to honor those works that captured that element.

The highly regarded English philosopher Roger Scruton said, "If you asked any artist, architect or poet prior to 1920 what the goal of their work was, the answer would have been to create beauty." Individuals from around the world recognize and comment on beauty. "It's beautiful" is a statement used to describe various items, events and situations. It is an intuitive response that implies inspiration, wonderment, awe and curiosity. It shows in sunsets, babies, marriages, broad views of mountains or oceans, flowers, and moments with loved ones and friends.

The Italian psychotherapist and philosopher Piero Ferrucci, in *Beauty and the Soul: The Extraordinary Power of Everyday Beauty to Heal Your Life*, said, "Beauty is a primary principle that touches all parts and functions of our being. It opens us

NI CAELORVM ✠ TV ES PETRVS
A FIDES
MVNDO

FIG. 1.3
CHAPEL AT RONCHAMP
LE CORBUSIER

to the world and brings harmony to our relation with others and with nature; it helps us reach out and touch the entire universe."

Our treasured works of art and iconic buildings are described as beautiful, and we protect and honor them. We construct museums to showcase them as valued pieces to be admired and preserved. We use them as touchstones and benchmarks against which we measure our own works, and they are destinations of our attention worldwide.

A stunning example is St. Peter's Basilica in Rome, often called man's most beautiful architectural achievement. With craftsmanship of unequaled beauty and skill, it lifts the spirit and confirms that awe and beauty are closely related.

The Mona Lisa is another great example of honoring beauty. It's regarded as one of the most beautiful and influential paintings in the modern world. The enigmatic smile on the subject's face has beguiled viewers and art critics for hundreds of years. An entire gallery is devoted to this painting alone, and the scholarship surrounding this single work of art makes it the most admired painting of all time.

The Chapel Notre Dame du Haut Ronchamp by Le Corbusier often is described as the beautiful and romantic anomaly in Le Corbusier's oeuvre. It springs from

FIG. 1.4
ROUEN CATHEDRAL
CLAUDE MONET

the ground with a poignant sense of sensuality and striking beauty. Few works in the 20th century have equaled the beauty of this structure.

The artistic works of Claude Monet often are cited as a sign that man is truly civilized. They often portray simple rural scenes with a layered sense of style and beauty that never have been equaled in oil on canvas.

Popularized by the movie, "Woman in Gold," (see image facing page one)by Gustav Klimt, the painting is a wonderful example of how beauty, inspiration and awe can catalyze and propel a lifelong commitment. It's a perfect example of how art inspires people to act. Often cited as one of the most beautiful paintings in Western culture, it was the central point of focus in a decades-long struggle to recover a misappropriated work of art taken during WWII and return it to its rightful owner.

Of course, these are but a few of the beautiful icons of our world. Each culture has its revered art and architecture, all seemingly different. Or so it seems. I believe most of our iconic buildings and works of art are based on the same set of patterns and ideals that developed over thousands of years, and reoccurs again and again in our most cherished works of art and architecture. Let's take a look.

2 | BEAUTY

BEAUTY IS…

Art and architecture — bringing the gods down to earth.

BALINESE EXPRESSION

Everyone wants to understand beauty.
Why not try to understand the song of a bird?

PABLO PICASSO

Beauty, like art, is a neurological activity, an urge for and feeling of pleasure emanating from the brain's lowest or most primal reaches…

HARRY FRANCIS MALLGRAVE

I am sitting quietly in the home that my wife Nancy and I built over 20 years ago. Through the French doors of the living room, I am enjoying the scene of peaceful openness that surrounds us. I am pondering a concept I recently had read in "The Aesthetic Brain" by Anjan Chatterjee.

The author explores the Pleistocene epoch, a period beginning some 2.4 million years ago. This is when the evolution of modern humans took shape. In particular, he describes how during this period, humankind came to associate the image of an open savanna with something bountiful, safe and habitable. Over time, knowing their offspring would thrive in this environment, the sight of such an open space and the recognition of the pattern associated with the savanna immediately would trigger physical relief in early humans.

Chatterjee, based on a 1992 paper written by Gordon Orians and Judith Heerwagen, asserts that the visual image of an open savanna creates a physical signal that became associated with survival and modulated subconscious human biology accordingly. Through the millennia, this reaction to the patterns imbedded in the savanna-scape became intuitive and influenced the neuronal growth of the primitive brain, effectively encoding intuitive reaction into our genetics.

I soon discovered there is extensive research to support the notion that people have multiple, subconscious tendencies toward their environment. Whether positive and supportive or negative and stressful, they are always intuitive. As Steven

FIG 2.1 | FALLINGWATER
FRANK LLOYD WRIGHT

An example of man establishing life within the savanna.

Pinker asserts in *The Blank Slate: The Modern Denial of Human Nature* (2002), "Our perceptual systems are designed to register aspects of the external world that were important to our survival."

Denis Dutton, in *The Art Instinct: Beauty, Pleasure and Human Evolution* (2010), echoes this notion, writing, "There are an infinitely large number of universal dispositions and behavior patterns — particularly persistent desires, motives, capacities, and emotions — that point directly back to the Pleistocene conditions where they first arose."

As an architect and artist long since intrigued by the impact of my work, this was quite a revelation. Visual patterns have the ability to trigger physical responses so powerful that they encode themselves in our genes. They become hereditary. I knew firsthand that visual stimuli, beautiful or otherwise, could elicit a physical response. But the idea that this response might become physically embedded and then passed on spoke to a much deeper suspicion I had had for many years. It resonated powerfully with a sense of enduring wisdom I had drawn from traditional architecture all these years.

In my quest to understand beauty in art and architecture, I never imagined how close the answer had been all this time, literally lying within us, in our biology. It was time for me to understand the biology of the subconscious mind in more detail.

At the most fundamental level, humankind is genetically predisposed to seek two things: survival and pleasure. Every day, our bodies process billions of actions without us even knowing it. All of them are geared towards these two goals. An amazing 95 percent of all actions processed by our brains are intuitive and subconscious, and all are geared to survival and pleasure.

To simplify a very complex situation, neuropsychologist Rudolph C. Hatfield, Ph.D., wrote in *Essentials of the Brain*, "Some anatomists prefer to divide the brain into three sections: the forebrain, the midbrain and the hindbrain." For this analysis, we will combine the hindbrain and the midbrain into one category, the ancient brain.

The ancient brain refers to the brain stem. Thought to have evolved during the Pleistocene period, it consists of the medulla, pons, thalamus and the midbrain. This is the center for our primitive and emotional responses — survival and pleasure — and is responsible for the more remedial, life-sustaining functions. It is here where the patterns of the savanna (safely spaced trees, open verdant countryside, water, food and shelter) encoded themselves to trigger a pleasure response.

Many other patterns also encoded themselves in the ancient brain through the millennia. Happen upon a large snake, for example, even for the first time, and we are intuitively alerted to danger, triggering a survival response automatically.

So multiple visual patterns built up in our ancient brain during the Pleistocene period that evolved into biological triggers. But what did these triggers do? How did these triggers affect our biology with survival or pleasure in mind? This is where the modern forebrain comes in.

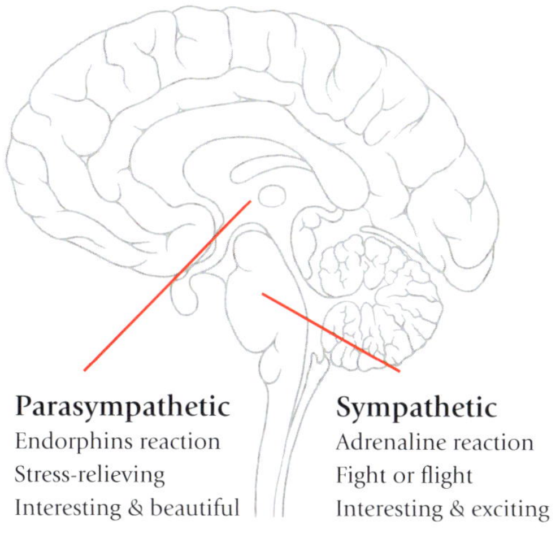

FIG. 2.2
THE AUTONOMIC NERVOUS SYSTEM

FIG 2.3

Our intuitive brain alerts us to danger before we are aware of its presence.

FIG. 2.4
THE MUSÉE DES CONFLUENCES

This building in Lyon, France, designed by Coop Himmelblau, is an example of fight-or-flight geometry. The architect is quoted as saying, "Ugliness is the next step in the pursuit of beauty."

Surrounding the ancient brain is the modern brain or, more precisely, the cerebellum and the frontal cortex. This is the center of rational thought. Judgment, reasoning, language and analytics originate in this portion of the brain. The modern brain is believed to have evolved during the Holocene period of the past 12,000 years.

The forebrain is responsible for higher-order cognition and consists of the limbic system, the thalamus, the cerebrum and the basal ganglia. The modern brain takes the information released by the ancient brain and converts that information to feelings, thought, memory and action. And where does the constant flow of information come from needed to feed the ancient brain and the modern brain? Our nervous system.

The nervous system is described as a system that collects information. There is a never-ending process of multidirectional communication going on between our brain and every cell in our body. These communication pathways are electrical and hormonal in nature, and together make up our nervous system.

Current thinking divides our nervous system into two distinct categories: the limbic nervous system and the autonomic nervous system. The limbic system is involved in motivation, emotion, learning and memory. The autonomic nervous system is responsible for control of the bodily functions not consciously directed, such as breathing, immunity, the heartbeat and digestion.

The autonomic nervous system is bifurcated into two subcategories: the "sym-

FIG. 2.5
SEVERANCE HALL, CLEVELAND, OHIO
ORIGINAL ARCHITECT: WALKER & WEEKS
DESIGN ARCHITECT: DAVID M. SCHWARZ ARCHITECTURAL SERVICES

pathetic" and the "parasympathetic." The sympathetic one corresponds with survival, and the parasympathetic one corresponds with pleasure.

When something triggers the sensation of imminent danger, the autonomic nervous system switches into sympathetic mode. It's sympathetic to the fact that all bodily functions and resources should temporarily be diverted to the muscle groups that will enable survival. This is the classic fight-or-flight or flight-or-freeze reaction. It is a danger signal that initiates the adrenal gland to release hormones to prepare the body, at the cellular level, for action.

Adrenaline and norepinephrine released during a sympathetic event raise your heart rate, narrow your mental focus and, in effect, put a person into survival mode. Cortisol then is released to signal the body to slow down bodily functions that are not immediately essential, such as reproduction, immunity and cellular repair. This all happens immediately and unconsciously. It is an autonomic response mechanism that emanates from the ancient, intuitive brain.

Following this activation, a rational reaction takes place in the cortex in the modern brain. This helps determine a course of action. How dangerous is it? What are the steps required for survival? What are the avoidance tactics necessary?

The sympathetic response is characterized by a sense of stress and danger. In contrast, the parasympathetic mode in our autonomic nervous system equates to pleasure. It is the stress-relieving and calming mode that results in our sense of well-being. Hormones such as endorphins, serotonin, DHEA and oxytocin change our cellular behavior. These chemicals are responsible for our feeling happy, wonderful, beautiful and inspired.

Importantly, critical functions involved in cellular repair occur when the autonomic nervous system is in parasympathetic mode. In this mode, our immune system is most available for action, and the body is able to defend and mend itself. It is not just a pleasure response. It is also a well-being and, as we will see in Chapter 7, a longevity response.

This analysis goes deeper than the ancient brain, however; it goes straight to the heart. It turns out when you say "follow your heart" that it is often an honest representation of your emotions and autonomic response. The neurological pathways through which the heart communicates with the brain are the vagus nerve, and the efferent and afferent nerves running through our spinal cord. Both pathways are a direct link to the medulla, in the ancient brain.

The heart's nervous system contains sensory neurites and local circuit neurons of various types, and these sensory neurites are distributed throughout the heart. They sense and respond to many types of biological information, including blood pressure, heart rate, hormones and neurotransmitters. With every heartbeat, a burst of neural activity is relayed to the brain, where this information is converted into neurological information. Then, this neural information is sent back to the heart to inform its performance. The heart is intricately linked with the state of our autonomic nervous system, and the differences between the sympathetic mode and the parasympathetic mode are quite significant and important to our well-being.

The heart dictates your emotional actions, which leads to one's feelings. This is known as bottom-up emotion tempered by top-down logic, which will be described in more detail in Chapter 6.

The point of this biological diversion is to demonstrate that humans, over millions of years, have evolved sophisticated and automatic response mechanisms that tie our cellular biology to our surroundings. In recognizing that visual patterns can subconsciously activate survival (sympathetic) and pleasure (parasympathetic) responses, we are confirming that art and architecture, because both at their essence are schemes of visual patterns, have an important role to

FIG 2.6
THE BEAUTY OF THE SAVANNA

"We respond to a broad and dramatic view as beautiful and inspiring as a result of 2.4 million years of evolution. We feel intuitively that it is safe, bountiful and full of pleasure"
— DONALD H. RUGGLES

play in our health and well-being. This idea will be developed additionally in Chapters 6 and 7.

Sympathetic and parasympathetic reactions emanate from the ancient brain. Neuroscience has isolated trust, loyalty and intuition in this portion of the brain. These are cognitive traits called emotions. Once the ancient brain is activated, it then activates the cortex or the modern brain. This is the center of rational and analytical thought, language, writing, learning and curiosity. These are cognitive traits called feelings.

"Emotions happen in the background of our consciousness. It is not until they register in the foreground as a feeling that we are aware of having an emotional experience. Feelings include fatigue, energy, excitement, wellness, sickness, tension, relaxation, surging, dragging, stability, instability, balance, imbalance, harmony and discord. Others are aware of these feelings by changes in our facial expression, body posture, the tone of our voice, etc. When we weep, others may wonder whether we are sad or happy, or just stressed out, but they can tell that we are having an emotional experience that has been translated into a feeling because we are displaying it" (*Architecture and the Brain: A New Knowledge Base from Neuroscience*, 2007, page 72).

Rita Carter points out in the book *Mapping the Mind* (2000) that our limbic neurological system goes through three stages in forming and responding to emotional experiences:

1. Creation of an urge with the intention of triggering action;
2. The action itself is endowed with pleasure;
3. Afterwards there is a sense of fulfillment or contentment.

FIG 2.7
THE VIRTUOUS CIRCLE
OF BEAUTY

Why is this sequence important? Humans are curious. We delve into the unknown with caution, but with unheeded thirst to understand. Why? We have to know. Professor Irving Biederman, with Edward Vessel, proposed in "Perceptual Pleasure and the Brain" (*American Scientist*, 2006) that humans have "an innate hunger for information: Human beings are designed to be 'infovores.' It is a craving that begins with a simple preference for certain types of stimuli, then proceeds to more sophisticated levels of perception and cognition that draw on associations the brain makes with previous experiences." Reviewing the sequence above: Step one is about curiosity. Step two is the pursuit of pleasure, and step three is the pleasure reward, i.e., contentment. It is the feeling of curiosity and the innate hunger for information that will lead us to beauty.

When we view a pattern that has the promise of beauty, it activates our curiosity and we turn our gaze to take a closer look. The parasympathetic nervous system then alerts the cortex that a pattern is in our view that registers in our limbic brain as safe and pleasurable. The curiosity leads to anticipation, which is followed by a release of endorphins. The feeling of pleasure is the reward from the endorphins. The result: the proclamation, "It's beautiful."

This leads to another cycle. Curiosity is activated even more, which leads to more anticipation, which is followed by pleasure, which initiates the proclamation "absolutely beautiful." And on and on the cycle goes. The more profound the pattern, the more curiosity and the more pleasurable the experience.

Professor Harry Francis Mallgrave, in *Architecture and Embodiment* (2013), defines it as: "Beauty, like art, is a neurological activity, an urge for and feeling of pleasure emanating from the brain's lowest or most primal reaches and associated with awe or wonder. And it is more than a passing fancy. When we taste a good wine, embrace a heartwarming friendship, enjoy the view from a mountaintop or succeed in our endeavor to elaborate upon the elements of a design skillfully, we feel revitalized. We feel a sense of happiness and harmony with the things around us, together with a sense of pride in our creative achievement. The world appears beautiful because we are experiencing a moment of flourishing or vitality, rather than mere survival. What biologists are demonstrating today is that there is indeed something substantive (electric and chemical) to the pleasure that we term beauty, something we can take to the bank. And this is indeed an impressive beginning because, if nothing else, a neglected artistic term has been reclaimed from somewhere in our historical past. Perhaps one day we may again feel free to employ the term with confidence and reverence. Perhaps one day architects may even occasionally condescend to use the term once again." (*Architecture and Embodiment*, page 51).

The view out of my living room, where there is such peace and quietude, returns to my consciousness. It appears to be so simple: Intuitive emotions generated by recurring simple physical patterns become feelings. I realize that the proclamation, "It's beautiful" is nothing more than a physical reaction to the recognition of a pattern that starts in our ancient brain as an intuitive emotion and ends in our modern brain as a physical feeling. When we experience beauty, it's the result of a endorphin release that has been triggered in the ancient brain that the modern brain consciously experiences as feelings.

The result of the endorphin release is a sense of contentment and pleasure. This is a powerful and compelling reward. I believe this explains why beauty is such a strong motivator and source of inspiration. It's so striking, we've given it a word: "beautiful."

This is a nontrivial departure from the idea that "beauty is in the eye of the beholder." It turns out that beauty resonates in all of us uniformly due to our common evolutionary history originating in the Pleistocene period.

The primacy of our pursuit of survival and pleasure is fundamental to understanding the important role that beauty plays in our lives. From the first moments of birth, pleasure is one of the primary motivators in life. It links directly with the genetic development of reacting to patterns such as the savanna environment and ultimately to architecture and art.

But what of these patterns? What might be their origin? How do they apply to art and architecture? What does this all mean and why should we care? All of these are important questions.

Yet, isn't something still missing here? Linking imagery and physical patterns with subconscious action is one thing. But when we experience beauty, it may start unconsciously, but it clearly ends up as something very conscious indeed. It is a visceral, physical feeling. The result is that it is often motivating. It inspires action. It draws us towards it in a bewildering, compulsive manner. This is the beauty that I have known. This is the beauty that we have strived to achieve in our work over the years.

FIG 2.7

THE 12TH CENTURY ROMANESQUE CISTERCIAN ABBEY OF NOTRE DAME OF SENANQUE, PROVENCE, FRANCE

NATURE'S BEAUTY

Stronger and livelier becomes my conviction that nature is the great antecedent of all our satisfactions. This has been so for many thousands of years.

RICHARD NEUTRA

We search for fractal structures to systematize ambient information. How we interpret these relationships determines whether we can successfully operate in our environment or not.

NIKOS SALINGAROS

To see the World in a grain of Sand
And Heaven in a wild Flower
Hold Infinity in the palm of your hand
And Eternity in an hour.

WILLIAM BLAKE

In the 1970s, while working for IBM in the computer research department, mathematician Benoit Mandelbrot discovered something remarkable. Mandelbrot was asked to solve a problem regarding telephonic transmission of data. The data graphed out in a similar sequence to a known mathematic problem. The known problem was called the Julia Set, one of the acknowledged monsters in math: Problems that were self-replicating with no apparent end. What struck Mandelbrot most was that the repetition was at every scale, no matter how varied he made it. Large or small, the graph looked the same.

From this observation, he wondered: Is there possibly some type of mathematic structure that might underlie the issue he was dealing with? For Mandelbrot, math was not purely a theoretical exercise. Rather, he relied upon visual criteria such as geometry to validate and even to initiate his intuitive leaps towards solutions. Thus, his recognition that the Julia Set pattern correlated with the pattern he was attempting to solve led to a revolution in the mathematic analysis of nature. This was the beginning of fractal geometry, a term he coined.

GRUNDTVIG CHURCH,
COPENHAGEN

Mandelbrot claimed that many patterns of nature are so irregular and fragmented that compared to Euclidian geometry, which is focused on smooth, regular forms, nature exhibits a different level of complexity. The existence of these natural patterns challenges us to study these forms that Euclid leaves aside as being formless and to investigate the morphology of the amorphous. Essentially he pioneered a way to find orderly patterns in disorder through mathematics utilizing a concept he invented: fractals. The key to this application is to understand that fractals are a self-similar pattern with self-referring redundancy.

The recounting of the discovery of fractals leads to an important realization about some events early in my career.

It was 1967. I was 16 years old. I attended the Expo 67 world's fair in Montreal, Quebec. I didn't realize how much this trip would affect me for the rest of my life. The best new discoveries from around the world were showcased in beautiful and amazing pavilions. A bewildering display of inspired creativity encompassing architecture, culture, technology and the arts was there for everyone to experience and enjoy. Upon arriving, my attention was keenly focused on the Biosphere, the U.S. pavilion. I had read that it was something special.

The arrival hall was quiet, and the procession through the deliberately darkened entry hall into the Biosphere was orderly and respectful. What happened next was unforgettable. It remains one of the most spectacular and wondrous sights I had ever encountered. Above me was the brilliant work of Buckminster Fuller. His geodesic dome was magnificent — ordered, mathematic, rhythmic, harmonious, resonant and beautiful. It was filled with light and the breathtaking, palpable tones of people from around the world expressing their awe. It was utterly inspiring and beautiful. I simply couldn't pull my eyes away from the incredible geometry of the dome. The more I gazed upon it, the more information I wanted.

Thinking back, it was a great example of a parasympathetic ordering of the physical world. I felt safe. I felt happy, connected and inspired.

The day wasn't finished, however. Nearby was another unique architectural event that I had heard I should not miss. The trip along the concourse through Expo 67 was eventful, festive and alive with friendly people from all around the world. The tram stopped frequently, and the ride seemed to go on and on.

FIG 3.1
BIOSPHERE, EXPO 67, MONTREAL

What seemed like a short distance on the map ended up being something of a wait. I had no idea what to expect, but my excitement and anticipation were building. Finally, the tram lurched to an emphatic stop and we exited onto a plaza full of people standing and looking up in awe.

Before me was yet another wonder of human intelligence, Habitat 67 by Moshe Safdie. It was the image of pure inspiration and beauty, conveying the sense of order, harmony and resonance. It, too, was special and unique. Once again, my eyes were fixated. Again, an insatiable curiosity had overcome me. The more I looked, the more I wanted to know.

After touring the complex with a guide supplying the necessary information, it was time to return to the hotel where I was to meet my family. As I was leaving, I walked some distance away to take pictures. Stepping back, I realized that Habitat 67 and the Biosphere looked similar somehow, but also completely different. Fuller's dome was ordered with a repeating pattern. Safdie's complex was

FIG 3.2

HABITAT 67 AT EXPO 67, MONTREAL DESIGNED BY MOSHE SAFDIE.

ordered with no repetitive order but with rhythmic order. There was a pattern linking them visually that was apparent at a distance and felt when up close despite the obvious stylistic and functional differences.

I since have discovered that the patterns in the works by Fuller and Safdie are categorized as fractals, defined by Mandelbrot as simple, self-similar mathematic themes developed and varied repeatedly to create a deep sense of layering. The more you look, the more you want to know. Nikos Salingaros and his close associate, Michael Mehaffy, have conducted extensive research on fractals (*Unified Architectural Theory: Form, Language*, Complexity, 2013). An underlying element of their findings is that fractals lead us back to our origin on the savanna and thus directly to survival and pleasure:

"The presence of complex ordered patterns in our immediate environment is reminiscent in some essential manner of the natural fractal patterns of the natural environment in which we evolved as humans. Those patterns are a necessary part of our experience and sensory grounding in the world" (*Unified Architectural Theory*, page 158).

"Math is our one and only strategy to understand the complexity of nature," notes Professor Ralph Abraham, UC Santa Cruz, "and with fractal geometry, we have a much larger vocabulary to read the book of nature." Math and geometry became the tools to analyze and reconstruct the natural world through the use of fractals. From math came 1) an understanding of the great harmony that exists in nature and how, as human beings, we are part of that harmony, not outside it, and 2) the ability to graphically depict nature's various patterns, especially with the development of powerful, high-speed computers.

Salingaros delves deeper into the definition as well: "Fractals are patterns or structures that are partly or entirely self-similar on different scales. Similar geometric patterns repeat at different sizes in a fractal. This means that fractals exhibit perceivable structure at every magnification. Some natural fractals such as fern leaves and nervous systems are ordered, whereas others such as coastlines and clouds are more random" (*Unified Architectural Theory*, Salingaros, page 156).

To understand the importance of fractals in our lives, it comes down to survival or pleasure. Michael Shermer, in *The Believing Brain: How We Construct Beliefs and Reinforce Them as Truths* (2011), states, "We are the descendants of those who were most successful at finding patterns. This process is called association learning and is fundamental to all animal behavior." One theory on the survival side is that we used repeating fractal structures in nature to determine the various distances that daily existence required our ancestors to negotiate. The result is our position in the landscape is perceived as safer and more secure because of the understanding of the immediate environment.

As for pleasure, fractals offer a repetitive rhythm that is directly related to our biological structure, thus the harmony one senses in viewing fractal geometries is one of the patterns that sparks a sense of pleasure and a declaration of beauty. Salingaros (*Unified Architectural Theory*) states: "I believe that architecture that is adapted to human physiology is nourishing ... it generates positive feelings ... through positive cognitive response to symmetries and fractal structures."

Taking this a step further, Ary Goldberger, a professor of cardiology at Harvard Medical School and a researcher into heart-rate variability, complexity and chaos theory, has proposed that fractals are intrinsically satisfying to the human mind. He says our mind responds to the complex, repetitive, increasing-decreasing patterns. Freed from rigid boundaries of scale, the mind can move inward or outward, up or down, at will. (*Healing Spaces*, 2009, Esther Sternberg).

FIG 3.3
FRACTALS

Similar geometric patterns repeat at different scales.

The fractal of a flower is a prime example. Who is not moved by the self-repeating beauty of a rose or the seemingly endless mathematical qualities of a beautiful tree?

Salingaros also writes, "The presence of complex ordered patterns in our immediate environment (today) is reminiscent in some essential manner of the natural fractal patterns of the natural environment in which we evolved as humans."

Repeating geometric patterns are rooted in nature and people have used them through the millennia as inspiration for art and architecture. These patterns, which people derived from the savanna, are in continuous use today. Some examples of this observation are shown here with the natural occurrence on the left and the manmade occurrence on the right. In each case, the manmade occurrence utilizes a pattern similar to the natural occurrence.

FIG 3.4 – 3.14

Examples of Nature Informing Design

FIG 3.4

FREI OTTO'S BUBBLE INSPIRATION | THE MUNICH OLYMPIC STADIUM ENGINEERED BY FREI OTTO

FIG 3.5

TREE BRANCHING | GAUDI'S SAGRADA FAMILIA, BARCELONA

FIG 3.6

BASALT STONE | CYCLADIC ARCHITECTURE, SANTORINI

FIG 3.7

HONEYCOMB | PLAZA DE ESPAÑA CEILING, SEVILLE, SPAIN

FIG 3.8

TREE ARCADE | MILDRED B. COOPER CHAPEL

FIG 3.9

SUNFLOWER | MOSTA DOME, MALTA

FIG 3.10

PEACOCK FEATHERS | KINGS COLLEGE CHAPEL, CAMBRIDGE

FIG 3.11

DAHLIA FLOWER | ALHAMBRA MACARABE, SPAIN

FIG 3.12

LEAF VEINS | JODHPUR, INDIA

FIG 3.13

BRYCE CANYON | OXFORD, ENGLAND

FIG 3.14

PALM LEAF | CALATRAVA'S PUENTE DEL ALAMILLO

Famed neuroscientist Dr. Erik Kandel of Columbia University states in *Reductionism in Art and Brain Science: Bridging the Two Cultures* (2016), that "the visual brain is a pattern-recognition device. It specializes in extracting meaningful patterns from the input it receives, even when the input is extremely noisy." This pattern-recognition ability, which we are born with, is critical to how we view, understand and manage our world.

Fractal geometry is an important component of those patterns. The utilization of grids and regulating lines by artists and architects as an integral part of the composition process is an example of how fractal geometric patterns can help order our sense of space to create the emotion of beauty. Concisely, we recognize the pattern and it results in pleasure.

Nature has been an inspiration and a source of pleasure for humanity for all time. Through our evolution, we came to recognize patterns found in our surrounding environment that either created pleasure or supported survival. Our responses to these natural patterns generated intuitive parasympathetic responses that resulted in the emotion of beauty. Those patterns that consistently generated pleasure were repeated through the millennia. Eventually they evolved to become important, recurring patterns in our artistic and built environment. That is a fundamental foundation of the theory of beauty as it relates to art and architecture.

Resonance, harmony and beauty are important concepts for our lives and neuroscience is discovering more about this every day. Recently in a paper presented by Alex Coburn, Oshin Vartanian and Anjan Chatterjee ("Buildings, Beauty, and the Brain: A Neuroscience of Architectural Experience"), they suggest that "attractiveness (beauty) is a key element in how the built environment affects our well-being." As we will show later in this book, our iconic works of art and architecture are often just intuitive variations of nature's patterns around us and within us. We also will show in the next two chapters that there is one single, ancient pattern that has been significant in the evolution of art and architecture. It is man's most profound pattern for creating beauty: the nine square.

FIG 3.15

ORNAMENTAL CEILING OF BORUJERDI HISTORICAL HOUSE IN KASHAN, IRAN

FIG 3.16

BOSTON AVENUE CHURCH, TULSA
DESIGNED BY BRUCE GOFF

This stunning example of art-deco-influenced architecture was created in 1929. It is laced with the nine-square pattern. It also repeats a pattern of 45°-angled forms at large and smaller scales.

4 | THE NINE-SQUARE MODEL

BEAUTY AND INSPIRATION

Neuroscience: "informed intuitions"

FRANK GEHRY

"Wholeness, life, has a way of being always simple. In most cases, this simplicity shows itself in a geometrical simplicity and purity, which has a tangible geometrical form."

CHRISTOPHER ALEXANDER

As architects and artists, we are in the profession of making patterns. A floor plan is a pattern. An elevation is a pattern. A painting is a pattern. Professor Don Hanlon of the University of Wisconsin states in *Compositions in Architecture* (2009), "The composition of a building is a set of patterns of various complexities organized one within another (and) all of the patterns relate to one another dimensionally to create a seamless continuum of scale and complexity."

A well-known and important pattern in the history of architecture and art is the nine square. As we will show in this chapter, variations of this concept have influenced and founded some of our most iconic and important works of architecture and art. Ascribed with cosmological significance in ancient Asian cultures, and representing the primal and perfect form of the world in the Middle East, it is a powerful example of the importance of geometry. This same pattern was used extensively in the Renaissance and neoclassical periods and, in some notable instances, it is still in use today.

Occasionally in one's journey through life, an idea presents itself that summarizes events and developments, leading to a turning point. It is a consolidation and simplification of many ideas, and a slowing down of the processing that leads to intuition. This is one of those moments. During the 50-year history of our firm, Ruggles Mabe Studio, encompassing thousands of projects, there is one pattern that is a recurring theme: the nine square. Somehow, through trial

FIG 4.1

A TARTAN GRID

Architects use the term to mean a division of varying-width spaces, made by lines crossing at right angles.

and error, we continued to land on this idea. We were not aware of this until a client mentioned that most of our projects had a similar quality. They described it as undefinable but beautiful.

We looked more closely. We looked back through our work of five decades and noticed some constants, all of which seemed to revolve around the nine square. It was fascinating how often it occurred, so much so that we started to look into where it occurred in other works by noted architects and in mankind's iconic architecture. This led us to look at mankind's iconic art. What resulted from these investigations was completely transformative.

Let us take a look at some of the basic patterns and variations that are derived from the nine-square pattern. Then we will look at how they apply to our iconic architecture and art.

FIG 4.2

APPLICATION OF THE NINE-SQUARE PATTERN IN A RESIDENCE, DESIGNED BY RUGGLES MABE STUDIO

FIG 4.3 | NINE-SQUARE

The Root Pattern

A simple grid with two horizontal and two vertical lines. The faded ends in this book's nine-square graphics emphasize the division of space over the containment inherent in the display of rectangles.

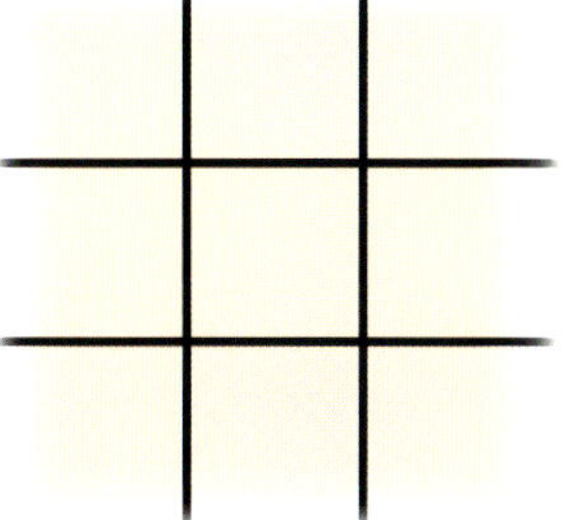

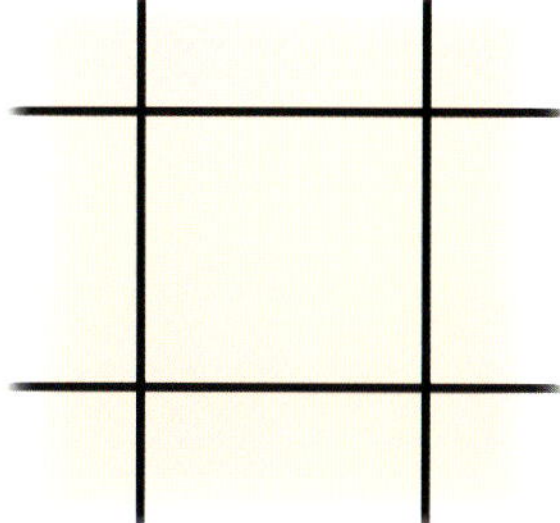

FIG 4.4 | DIVIDING SPACE

Division, Not Squares

"Nine square" is a well-established term in architecture. But it does not strictly demand squares. It is about the division of space. It requires two vertical divisions and two horizontal divisions.

FIG 4.5 | SEEING THE PATTERN

Subtle But Powerful

The designer uses the pattern. The viewer may not see it but can usually feel it.

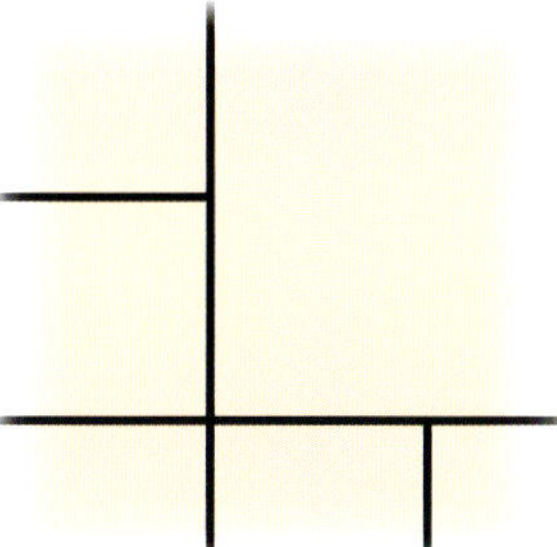

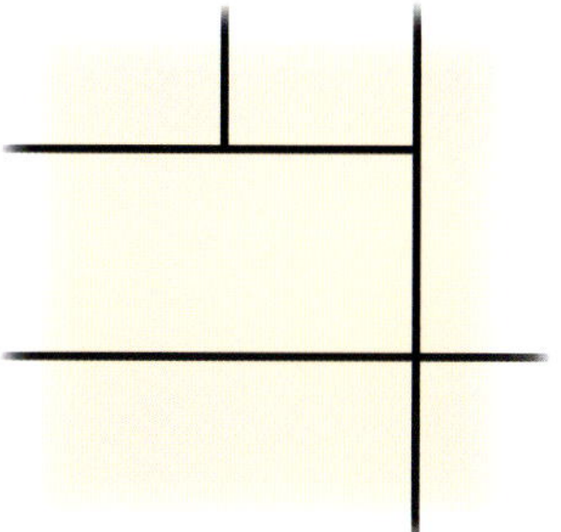

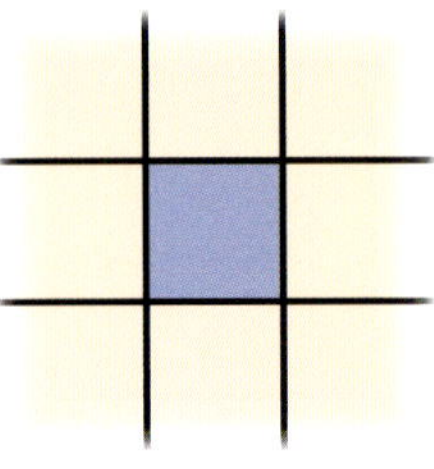

FIG 4.6 | NINE SQUARE

With an emphasis on the crossing pattern, it becomes a center-focused organization, evident in examples like Barcelona's block plan by Cerda and a singular window with a strong border.

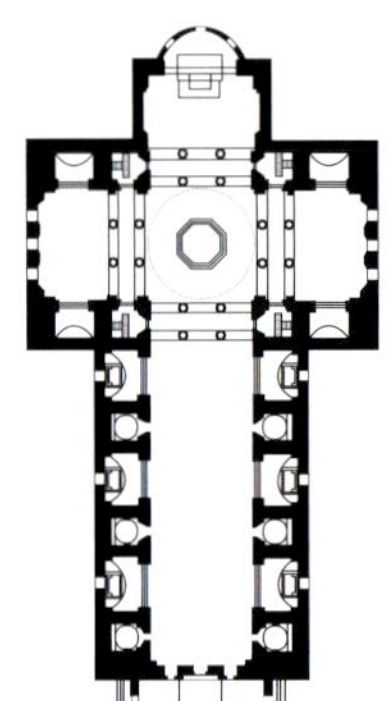

FIG 4.7 | NINE-SQUARE EXTENSIONS

The addition of extensions to the center of the crossing pattern gives emphasis to circulation, and can be seen in such examples as the Latin cross plan of a church seen here in the Basilica of San Andrea and in the Ibaraki Kasugaoka Church, designed by Tadao Ando.

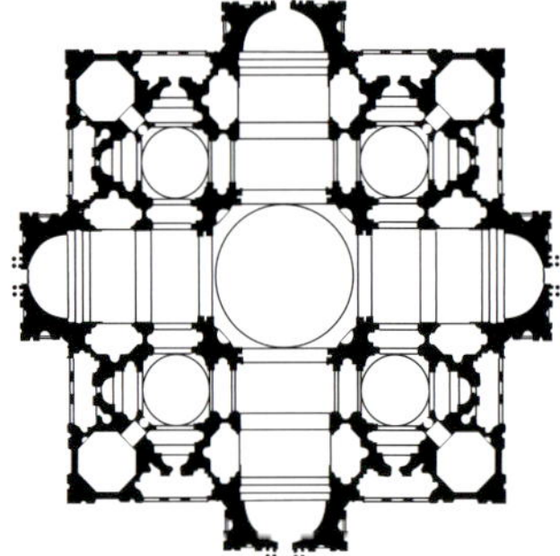

FIG 4.8 | NINE-SQUARE CLUSTER

A variation on the crossing pattern creates a cluster effect that can be seen in the Basilica of St. Peter in Rome and in the stone-carved lattice work in the windows of Fort Chittorgarh in India.

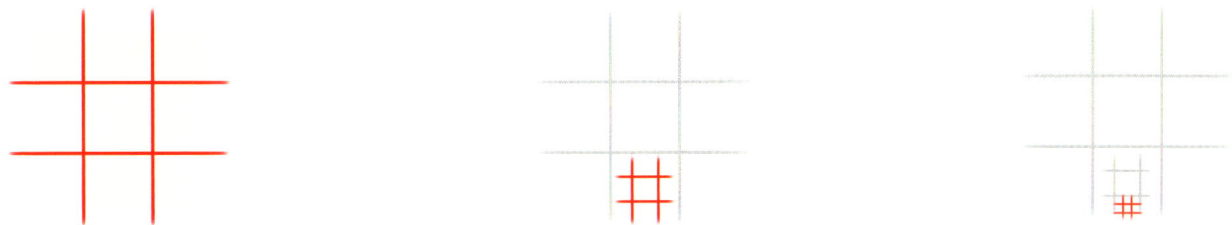

FIG 4.9 | THE FRACTAL'S HABIT OF DESCENDING SCALE

Introducing a fractal component to the nine square with self-similar geometry and a descending scale gives depth to the pattern, and shows that it operates on multiple scales simultaneously.

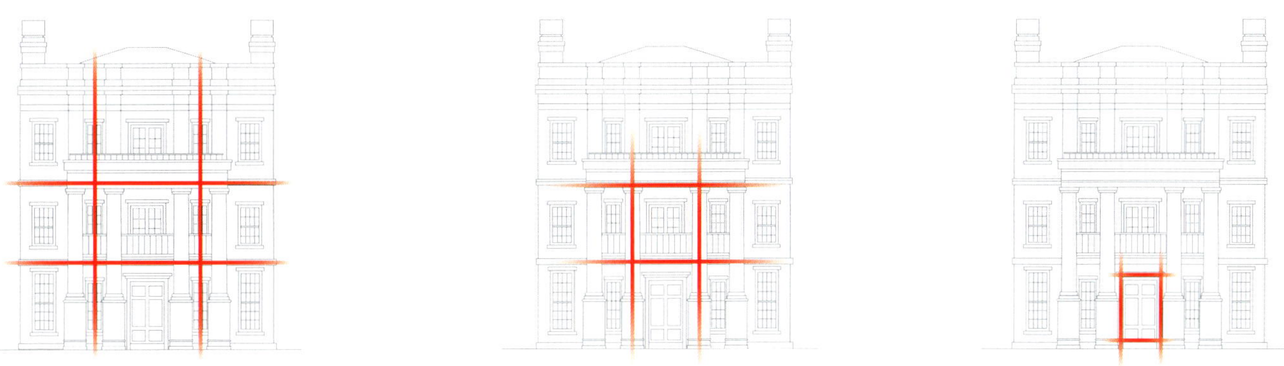

FIG 4.10 | APPLIED TO A TOWNHOME

Applying this idea to the front facade of a classical townhome, we can see that the nine-square grid is present over the entire building, portico and front door.

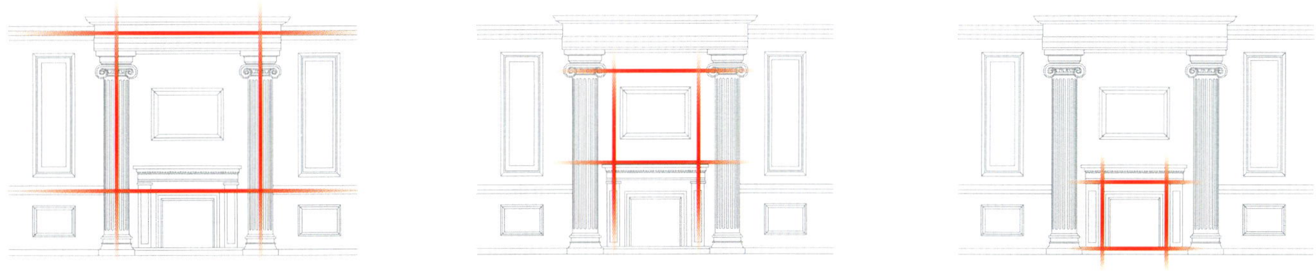

FIG 4.11 | APPLIED TO THE INTERIOR

The grid is applicable even in the interior of a space. Here it is first applied to the overall wall, next to the interior columns and finally, a detail such as a fireplace.

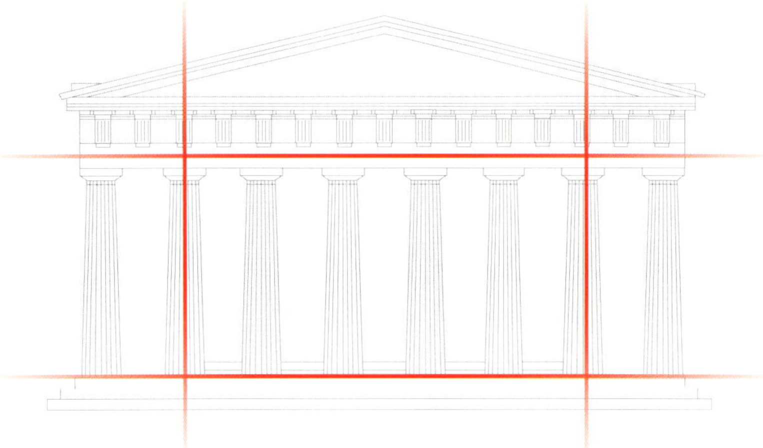

FIG 4.12 | THE PARTHENON

The Parthenon was built by the ancient Greeks in Athens between 447 and 438 B.C. It is regarded as one of the most carefully proportioned buildings ever. It was constructed using lines that were not exactly parallel to make it appear more visually appealing from the front-entrance perspective. The tapering of the columns is based on proportions of the human body.

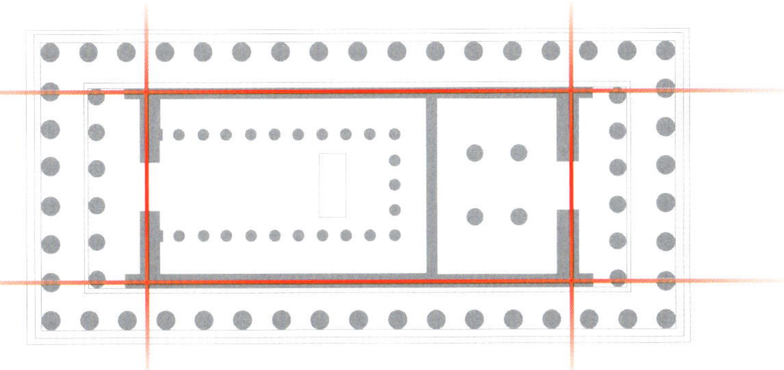

FIG 4.13 | THE PLAN

The nine-square grid encapsulates the entire plan. The vertical axes are created by the two outer entrances, and the horizontal axes by the outer walls.

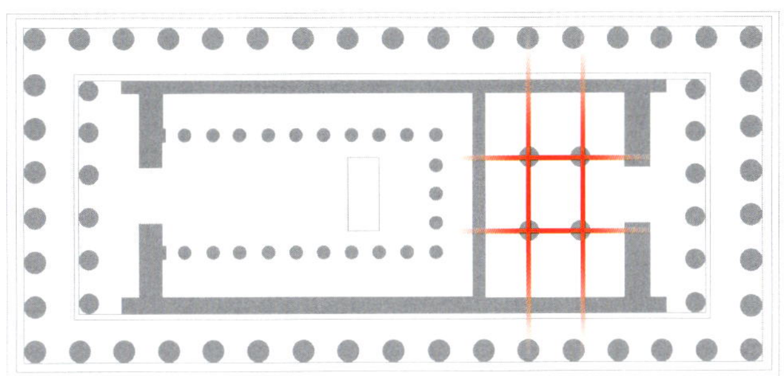

FIG 4.14 | THE ADYTON

Within the building, the four main columns of the room clearly dictate the cross axis of the nine-square composition used to form the adyton.

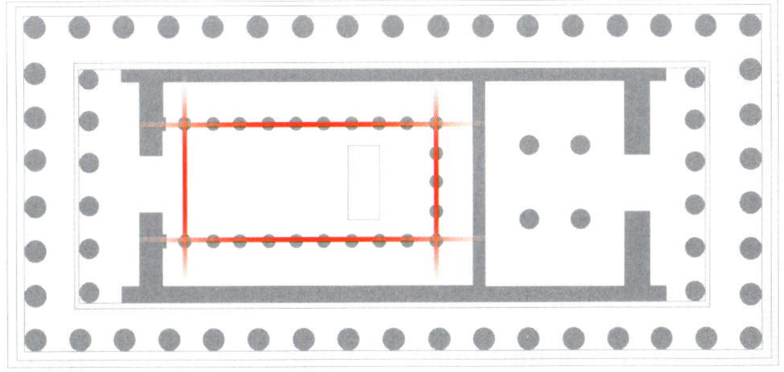

FIG 4.15 | THE NAOS

To the east, the pattern is formed by the columns near the edges of the room, the east doorway wall and the entry gallery. The space is centered horizontally around the statue of Athena. The statue center is farther back in the room to emphasize inward movement and create a procession.

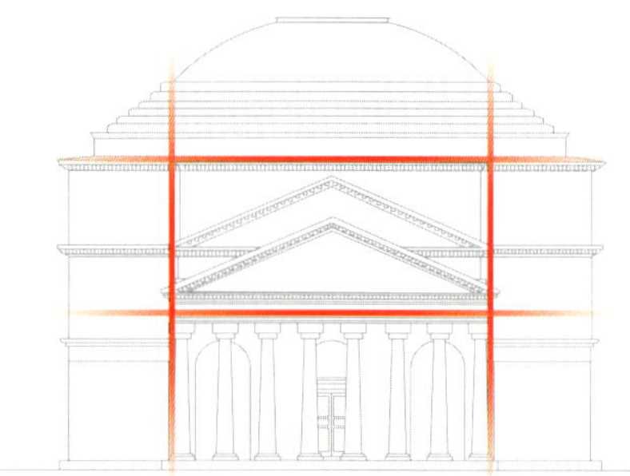

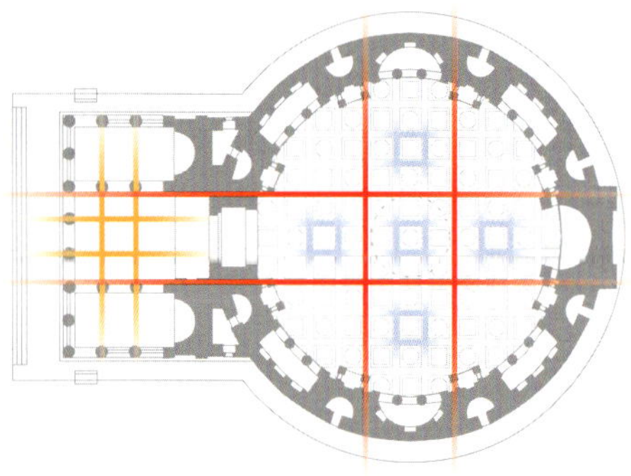

FIGS. 4.16 | THE PANTHEON

One of the most beautiful and revered buildings in Western history is the Pantheon. While the exact age of the iconic structure is unknown, it is thought to have been built around 120 A.D by Emperor Hadrian and architect Apollodorus of Damascus. To this day the structure remains the largest unsupported dome in the world. Its diameter and height are equal (142 feet). In elevation, this symmetry can be seen, and the nine-square grid divides the space. In the plan there are two nine-square grids, one at the entrance and one over the main plan, with diagonal symmetry.

FIG. 4.17 | THE TAJ MAHAL

The famous Taj Mahal (1628-1658) was designated a UNESCO World Heritage Site in 1983 for being "the jewel of Muslim art" in India and one of the universally admired masterpieces of the world's heritage. It was recently declared a winner of the New 7Wonders of the World initiative. Using the same metrics, the analysis shows a strong base, a body and a crown horizontally, and three distinct masses that form the body vertically. Be sure to notice the window grid in the center bay, which sets off the beginnings of a fractal component.

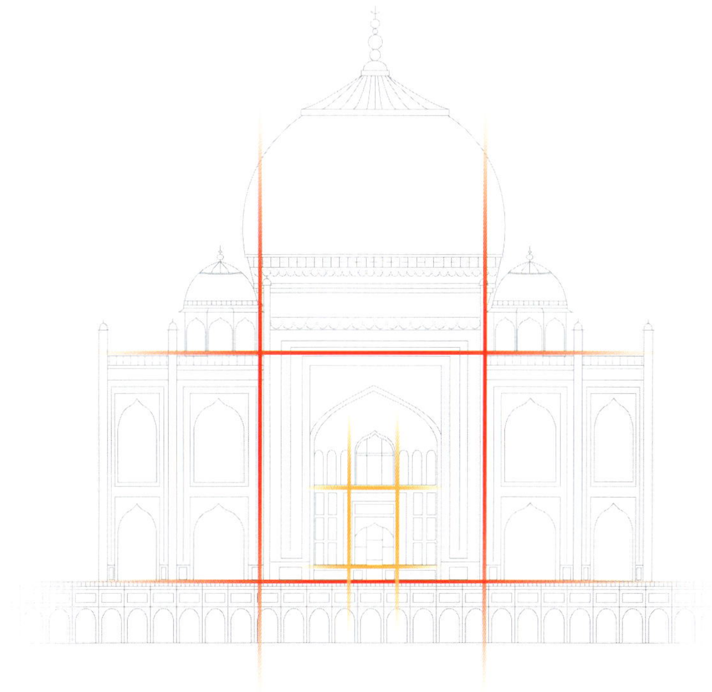

FIG 4.18 | NOTRE DAME DE PARIS

Another World Heritage site, Notre Dame de Paris is often listed as the most beautiful example of Gothic cathedral design in France. It's a veritable symphony of nine square.

FIG. 4.19 | PALLADIO'S VILLA ROTONDA

Andrea Palladio's work is generally considered some of the most seminal and beautiful ever produced by an architect. His work, rooted deeply in the patterns that he took from the Roman Forum and utilized to his own ends, was based almost entirely on the nine-square pattern. Here is a plan of one of his most famous works, Villa Rotonda. It is the very definition of a nine-square pattern.

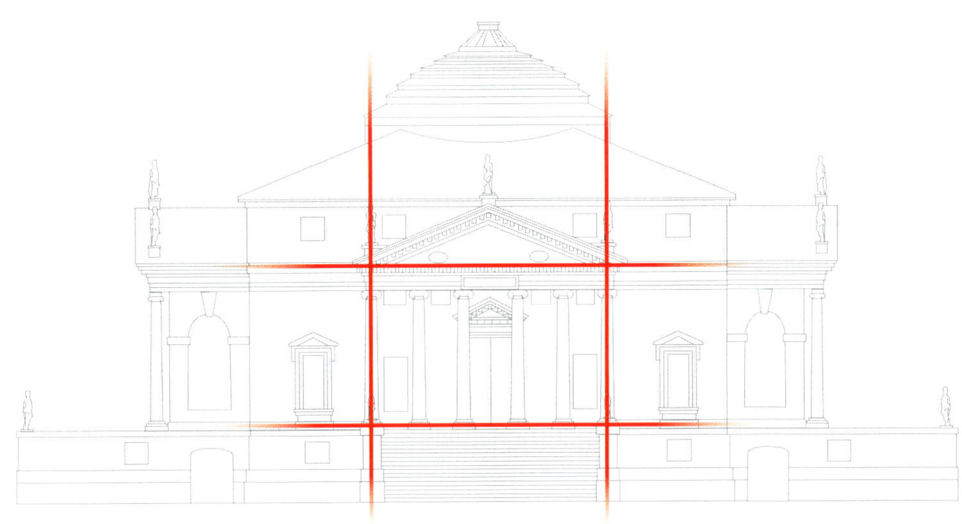

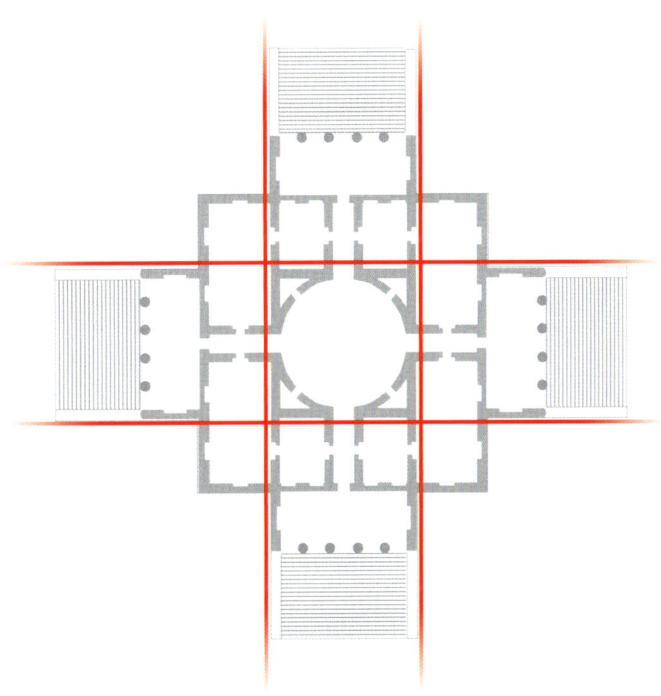

FIG. 4.20 | BYODO-IN TEMPLE

At the foot of the Ko'olau Mountains, in Valley of the Temples Memorial Park, rests the noble Byodo-In Temple. The 950-year-old temple is a United Nations World Heritage Site in Uji, Japan. It was built in the Heian period as a rural villa and thousands visit the historic site each year, seeking beauty and peace. The nine-square grid is most apparent in the central piece of the structure. The vertical lines are dictated by the edge columns while the horizontal lines originate from the two levels of roof. It is a magnificent example of beauty and cultural preservation.

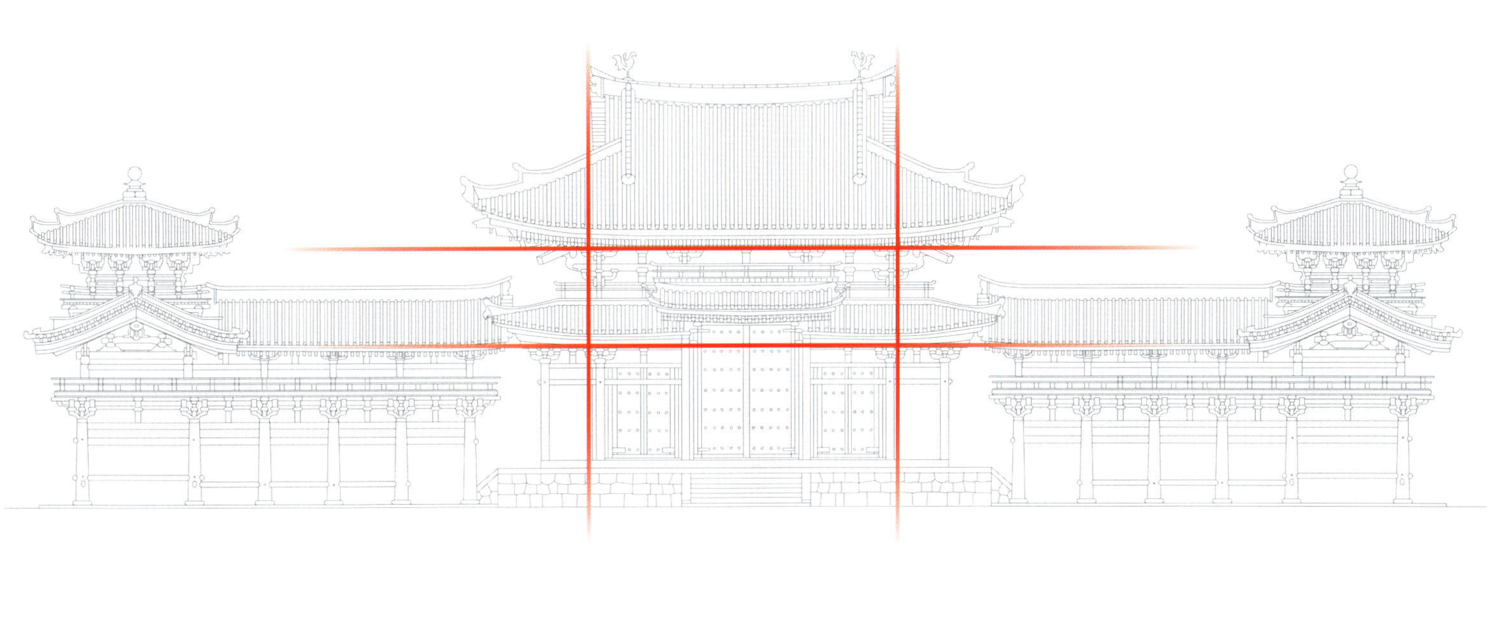

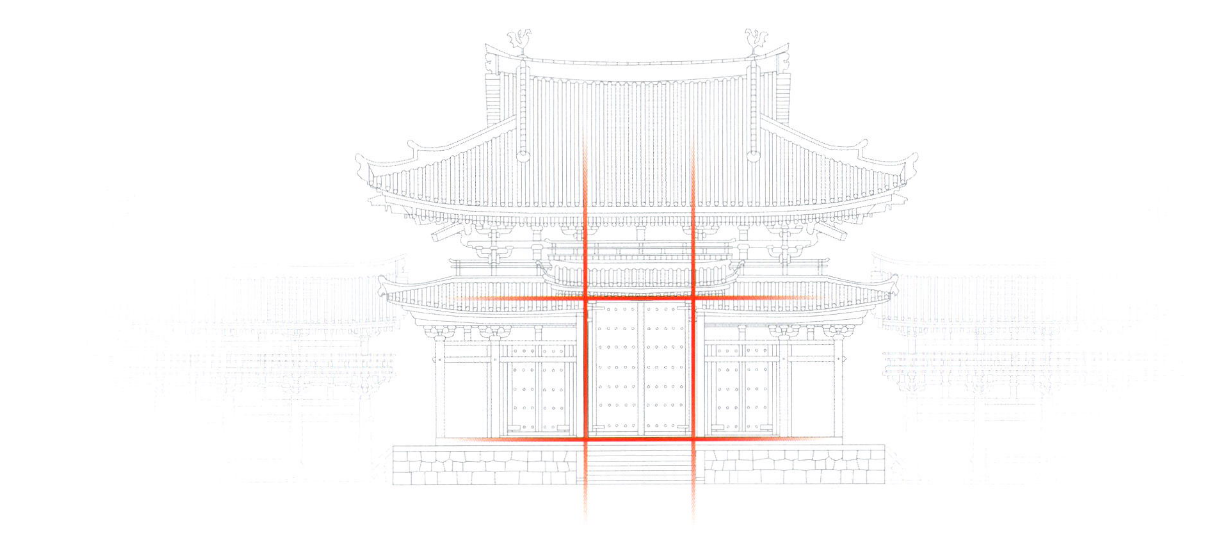

FIG. 4.21 | ST. PETER'S BASILICA, ROME

Another UNESCO World Heritage Site, Saint Peter's Basilica in Rome, Italy, was described by Ralph Waldo Emerson as "an ornament of the earth … the sublime of the beautiful." It was designed by Bramante, Michelangelo, Paderno and Bernini, and constructed between 1506 and 1626. The complete plan of the Basilica and Piazza shows the utilization of the nine-square pattern for organization of the individual components.

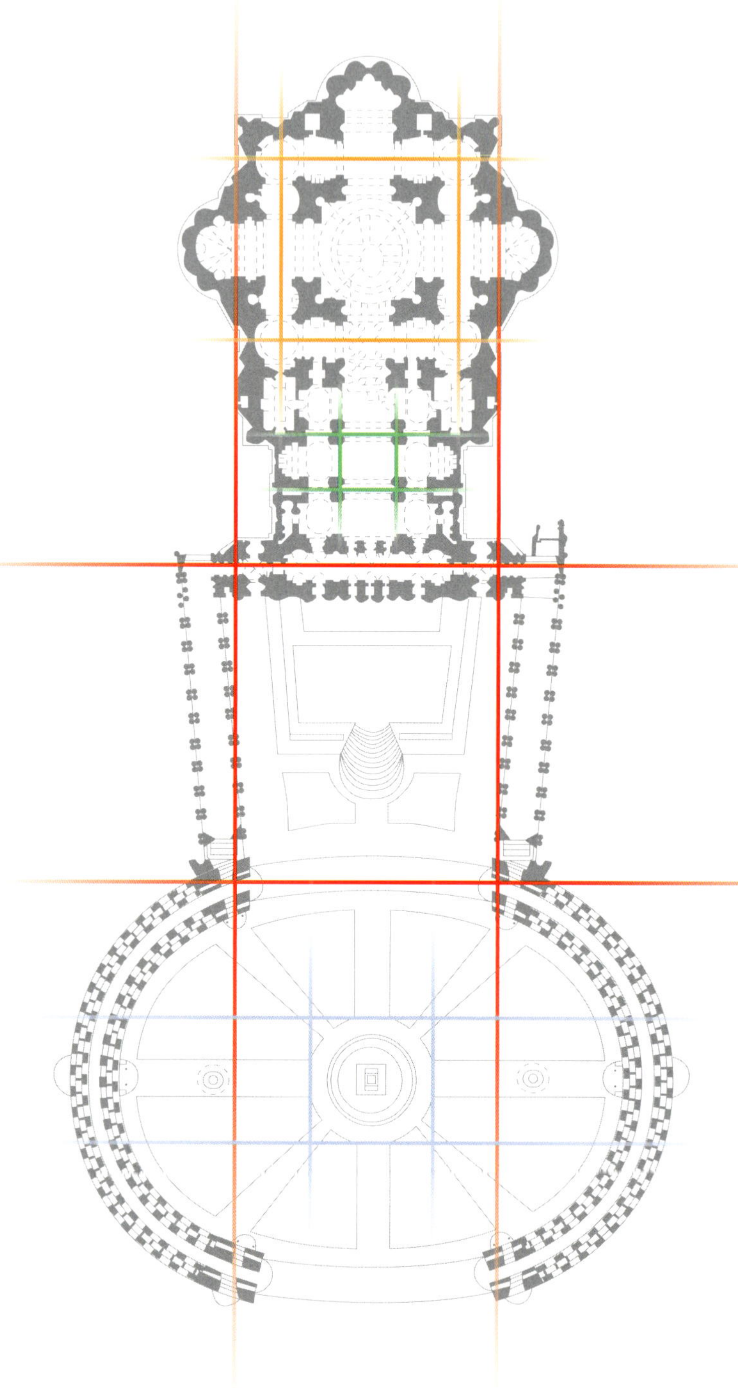

IN HONOREM PRINCIPIS APOST PAVLVS V BVRG
VS ROMANVS PONT MAX AN MDCXII PONT VII

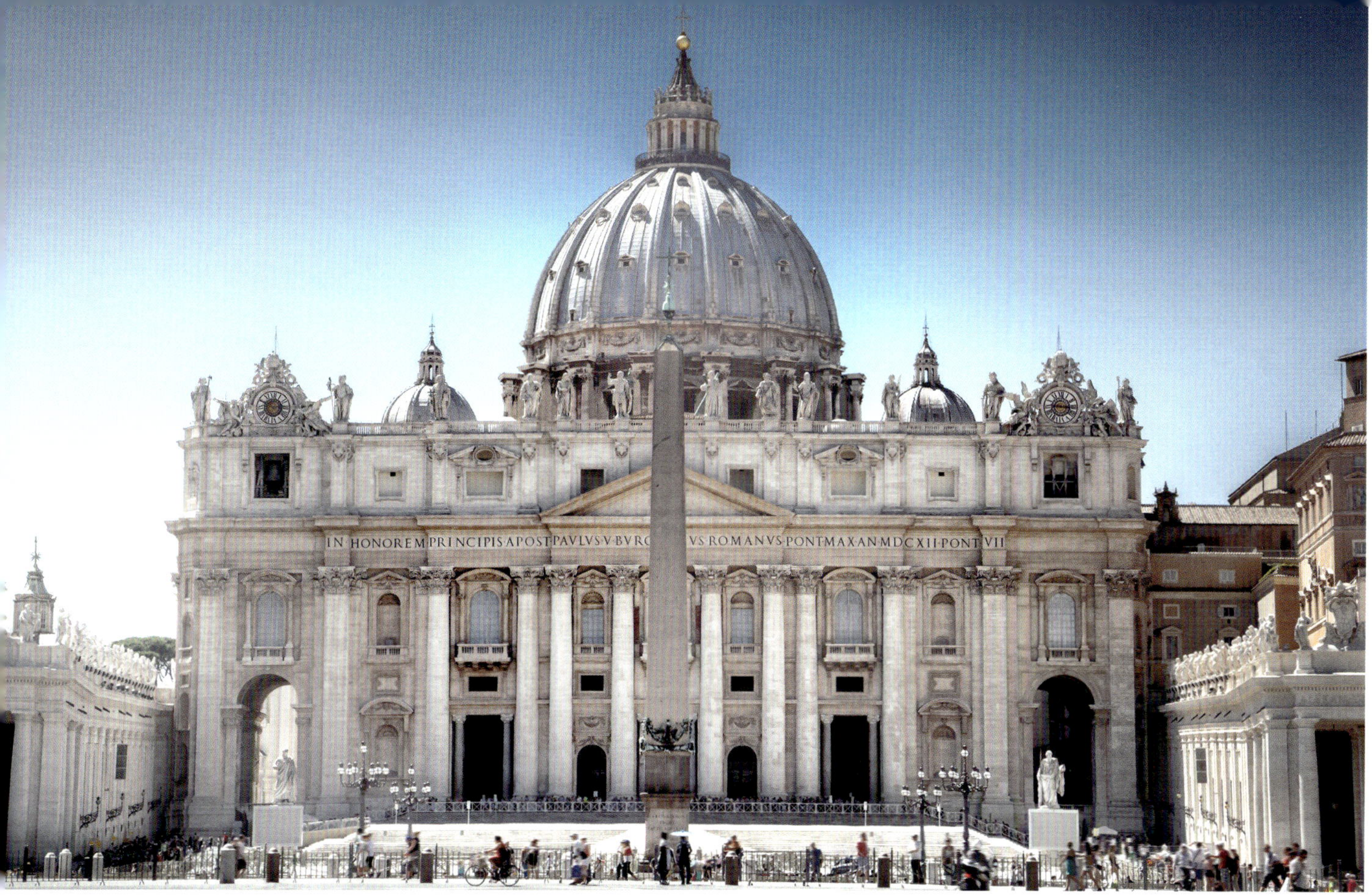

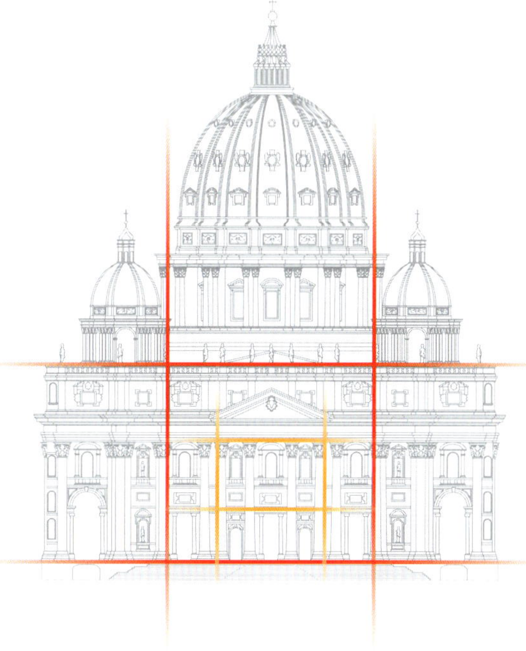

FIG. 4.22 | US CAPITOL BUILDING

The Capitol Building of the United States has been declared a National Historic Landmark by the National Park Service and was listed as No. 6 on the American Institute of Architects' "America's Favorite Architecture" list. An analysis of the west elevation finds many possible combinations of the nine-square pattern. The entire composition is a nine-square fractal. Two examples are shown here.

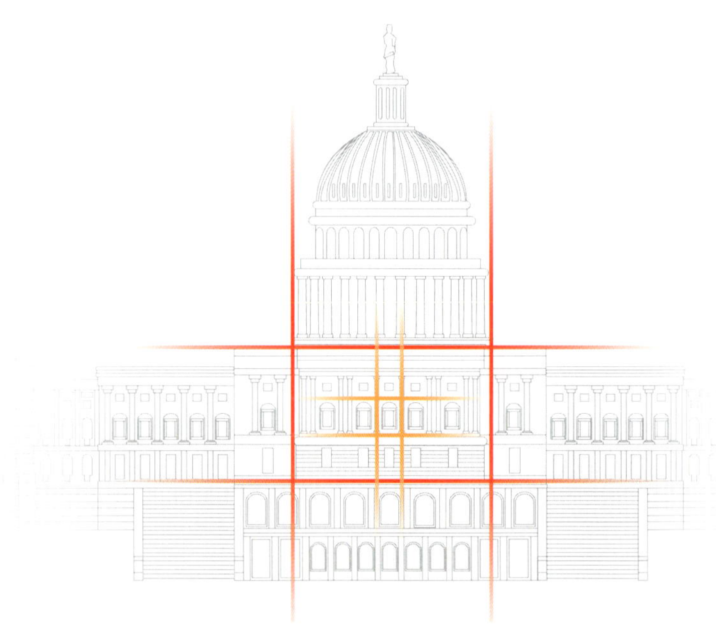

FIG. 4.23 | MONTICELLO

Monticello in Charlottesville, Virginia, designed by Thomas Jefferson, is the only private home in the world to be designated a UNESCO World Heritage Site. The design was influenced by the works of Andrea Palladio. Jefferson utilized the nine-square fractal pattern to great effect. It's often cited as one of America's most beautiful and admired architectural sites.

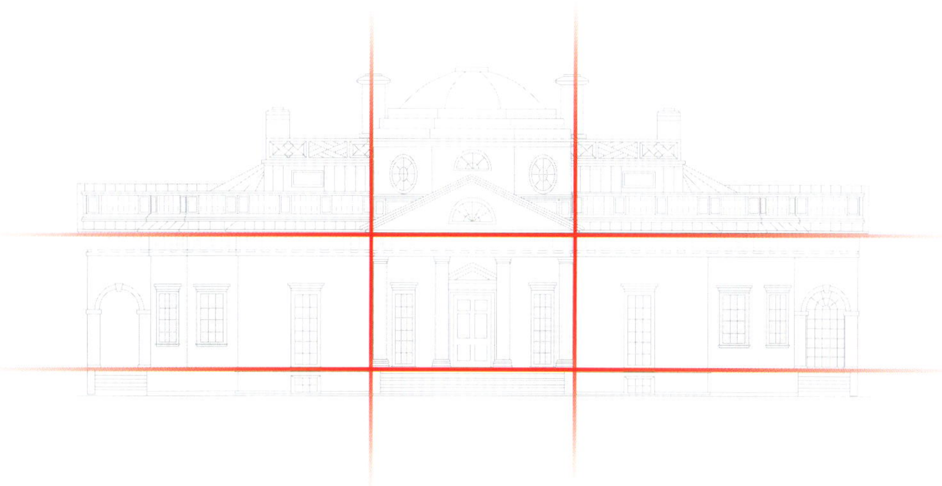

FIG. 4.24 | FALLINGWATER

Selected to be included on the World Heritage List by the UNESCO World Heritage Committee, Fallingwater is considered the most famous and beautiful home in America. Frank Lloyd Wright's utilization of the nine square was an important part of his early work, and it resurfaces in the organizational concept for the cross section of the home.

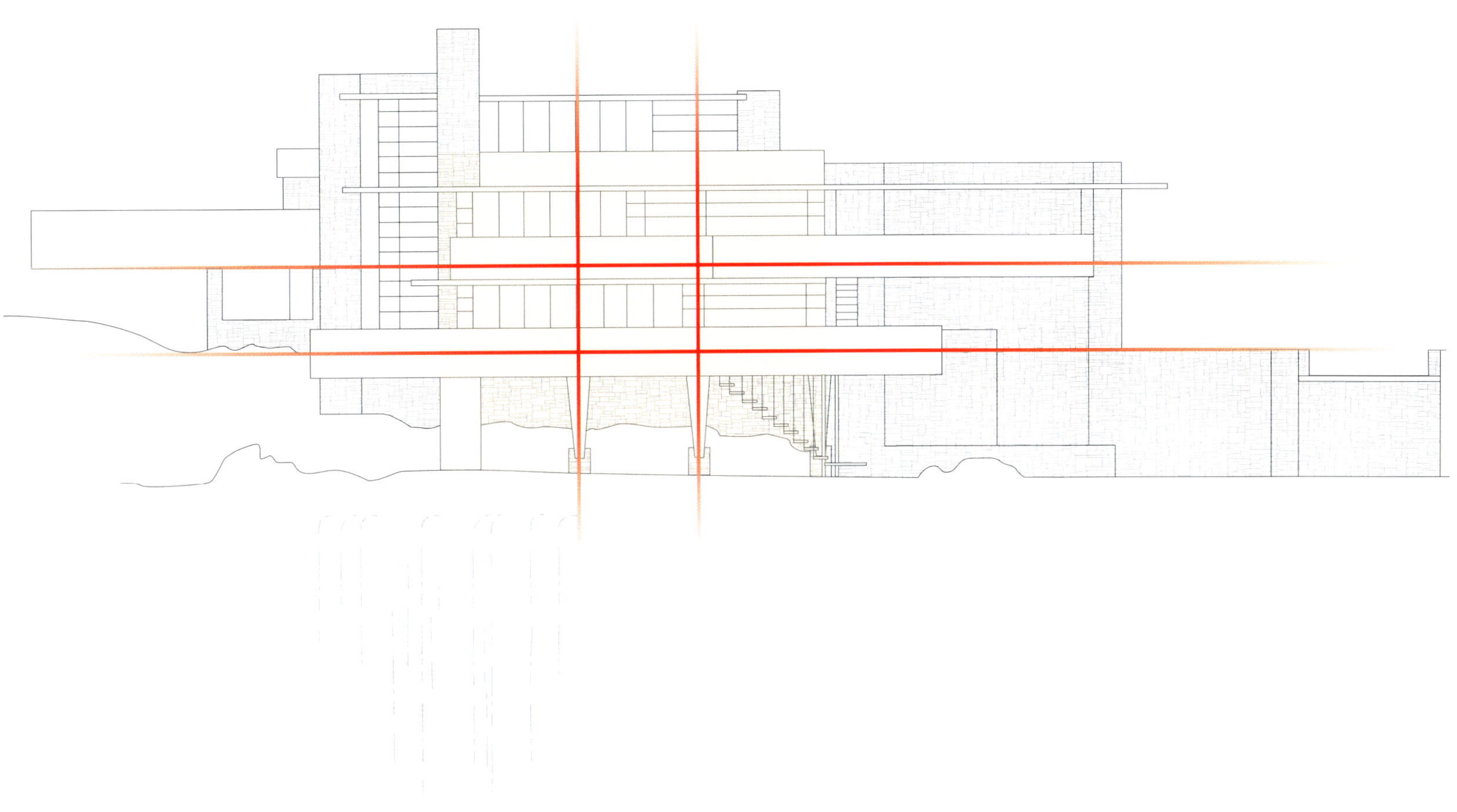

FIG. 4.25 | THE FARNSWORTH HOUSE

Mies Van der Rohe's masterpiece, the Farnsworth House located in Plano, Illinois, is a National Historic Landmark. Architectural writer Paul Goldberger recently deemed it a "masterpiece of modern architecture for its timeless beauty." The composition of the elevation shows how the tartan nine-square pattern can apply to a minimalist composition. Van der Rohe, due to classic training early in his career, clearly understood the importance of this pattern and utilized it throughout his work.

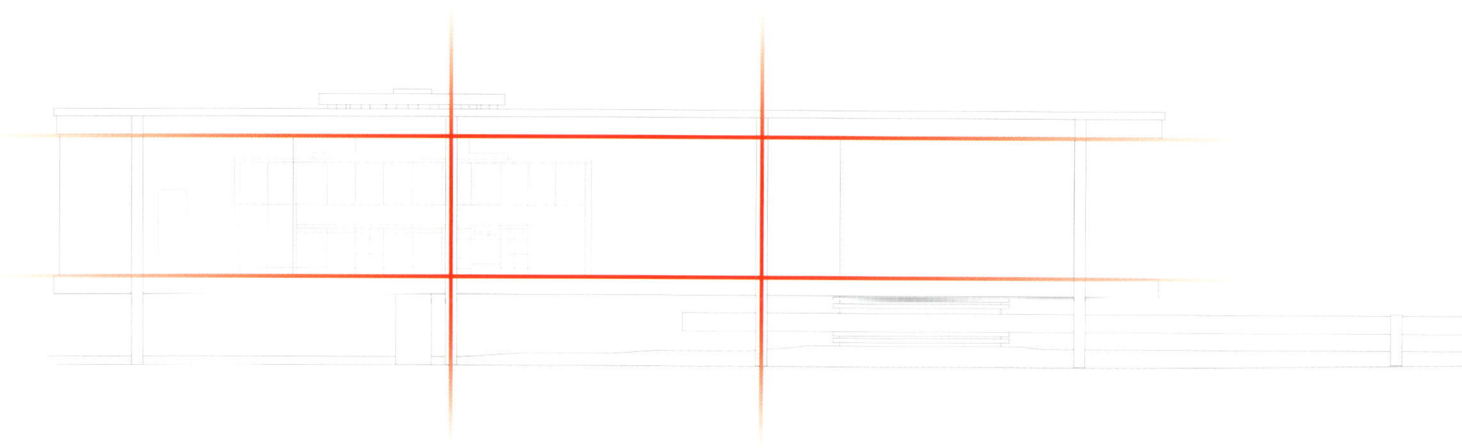

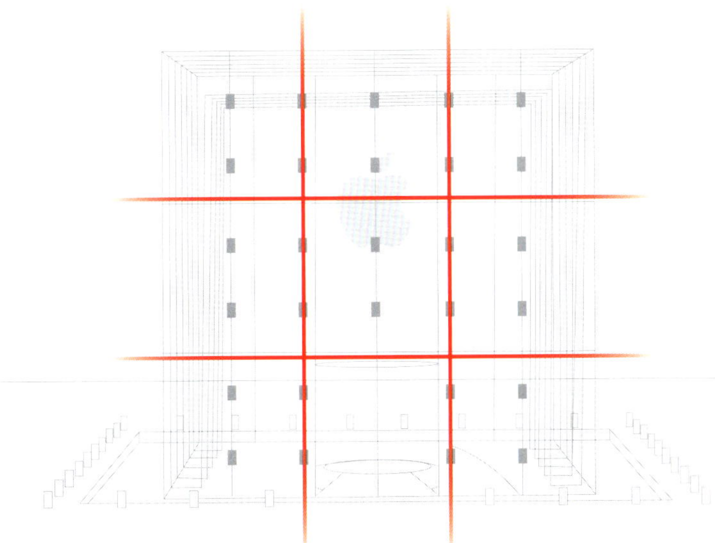

FIG. 4.26 | APPLE STORE, NEW YORK

A more recent example of applying the nine-square pattern to achieve a timeless sense of beauty and creating a rich internal environment is the Apple store in New York, designed by Bohlin Cywinski Jackson. Apple utilizes the nine-square model throughout its store designs, and this is perhaps the most striking example.

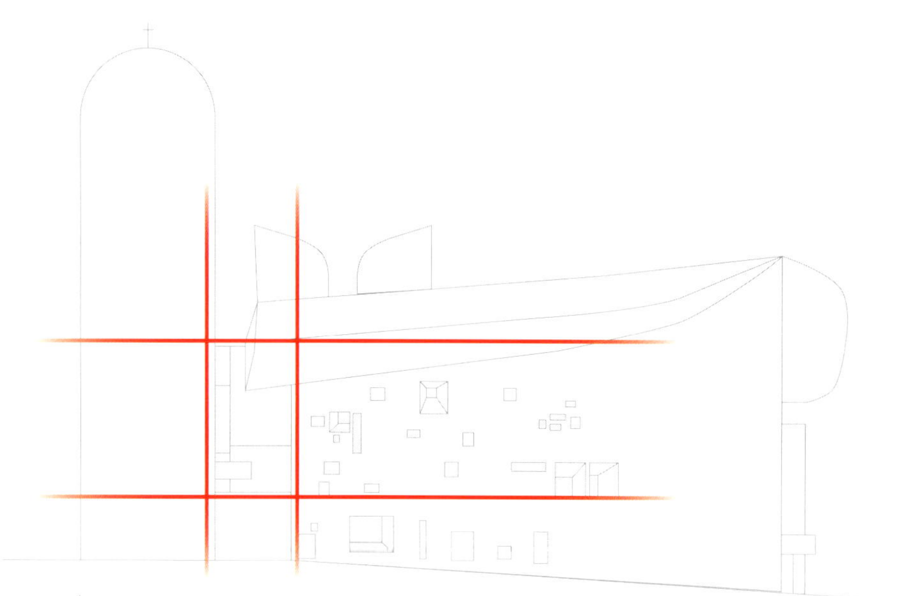

FIG. 4.27| RONCHAMP

An acclaimed master of contemporary architecture, Le Corbusier was trained in the classics as well and utilized the nine-square pattern throughout his career. The Chapel of Notre Dame du Haut is perhaps his most beautiful work. This building also is listed as a UNESCO World Heritage Site and is considered an outstanding contribution to the Modern Movement.

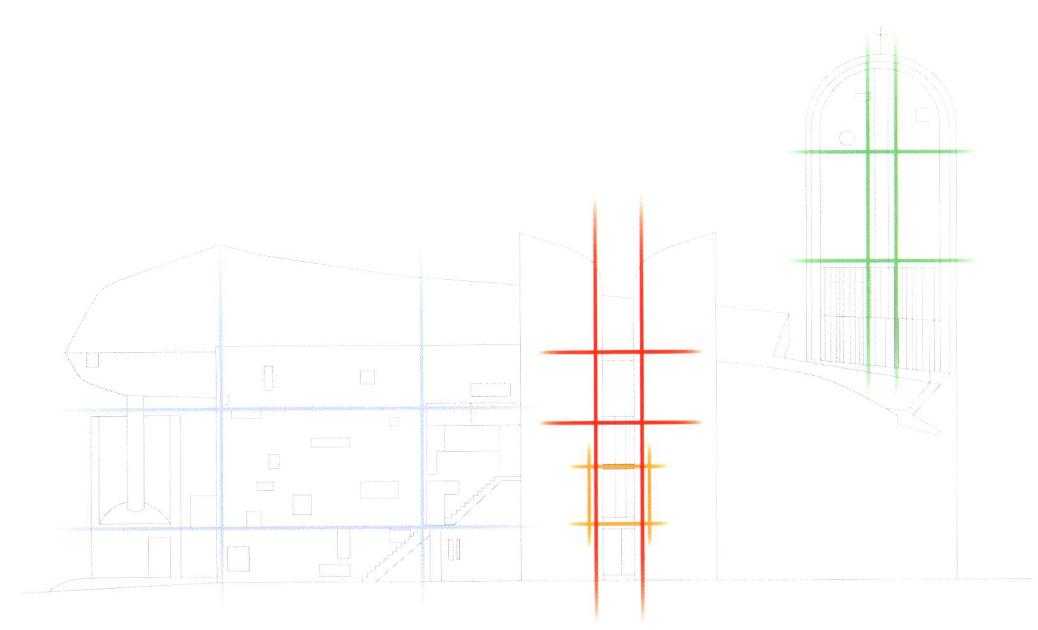

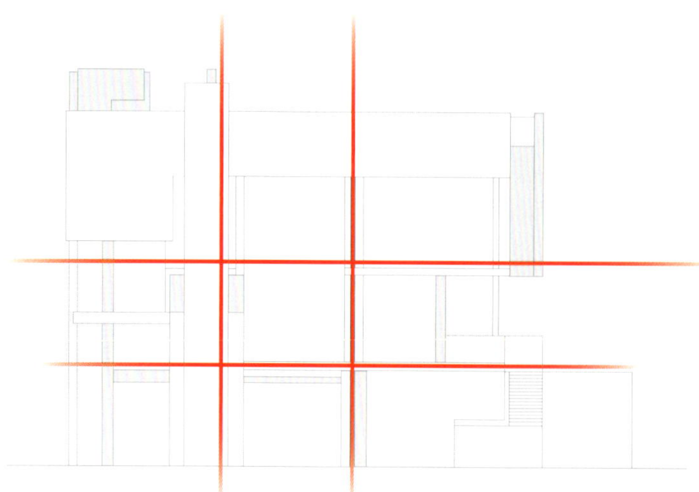

FIG. 4.28 | FREDERICK J. SMITH RESIDENCE

Richard Meier created the Frederick J. Smith residence in 1965 following the principles of Le Corbusier and blending them with his unique stylistic approach. The home was awarded the Twenty-Five Year Award from the American Institute of Architects.

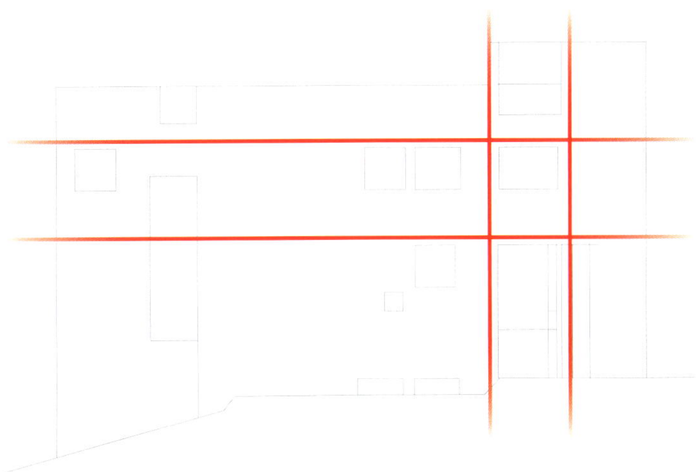

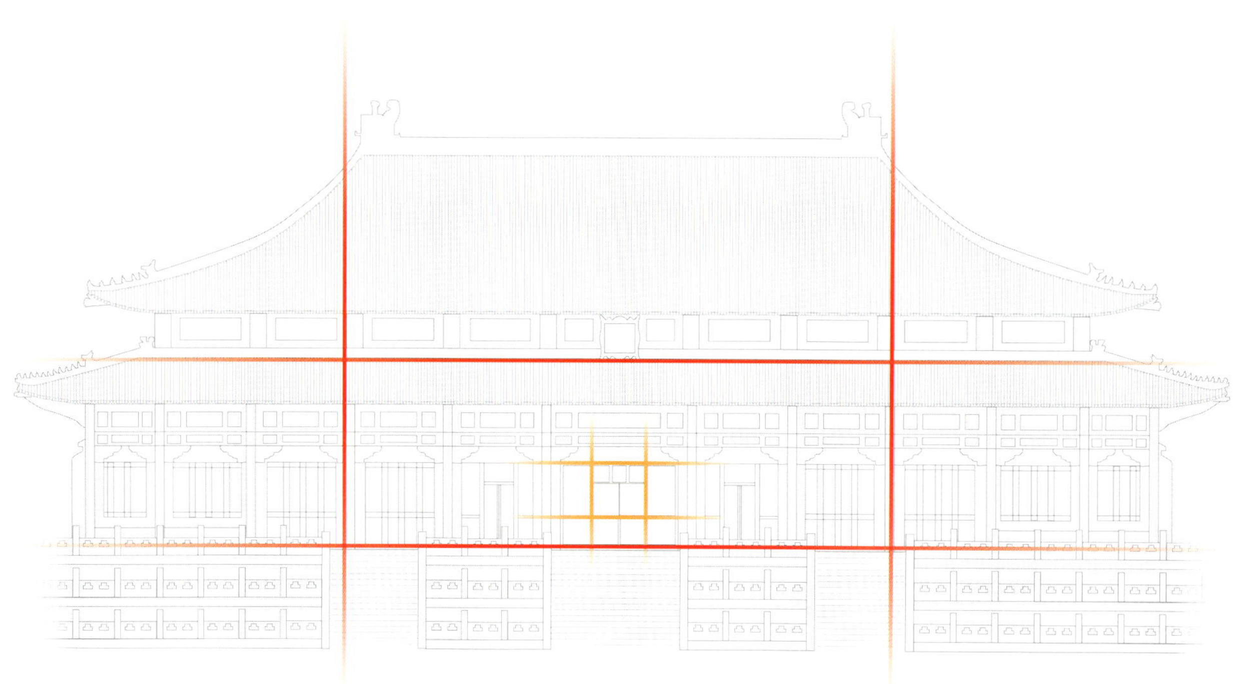

FIG 4.29 | THE FORBIDDEN CITY, BEIJING

The Forbidden City in Beijing, China, was built in1420 and contains a plethora of nine-square grids.

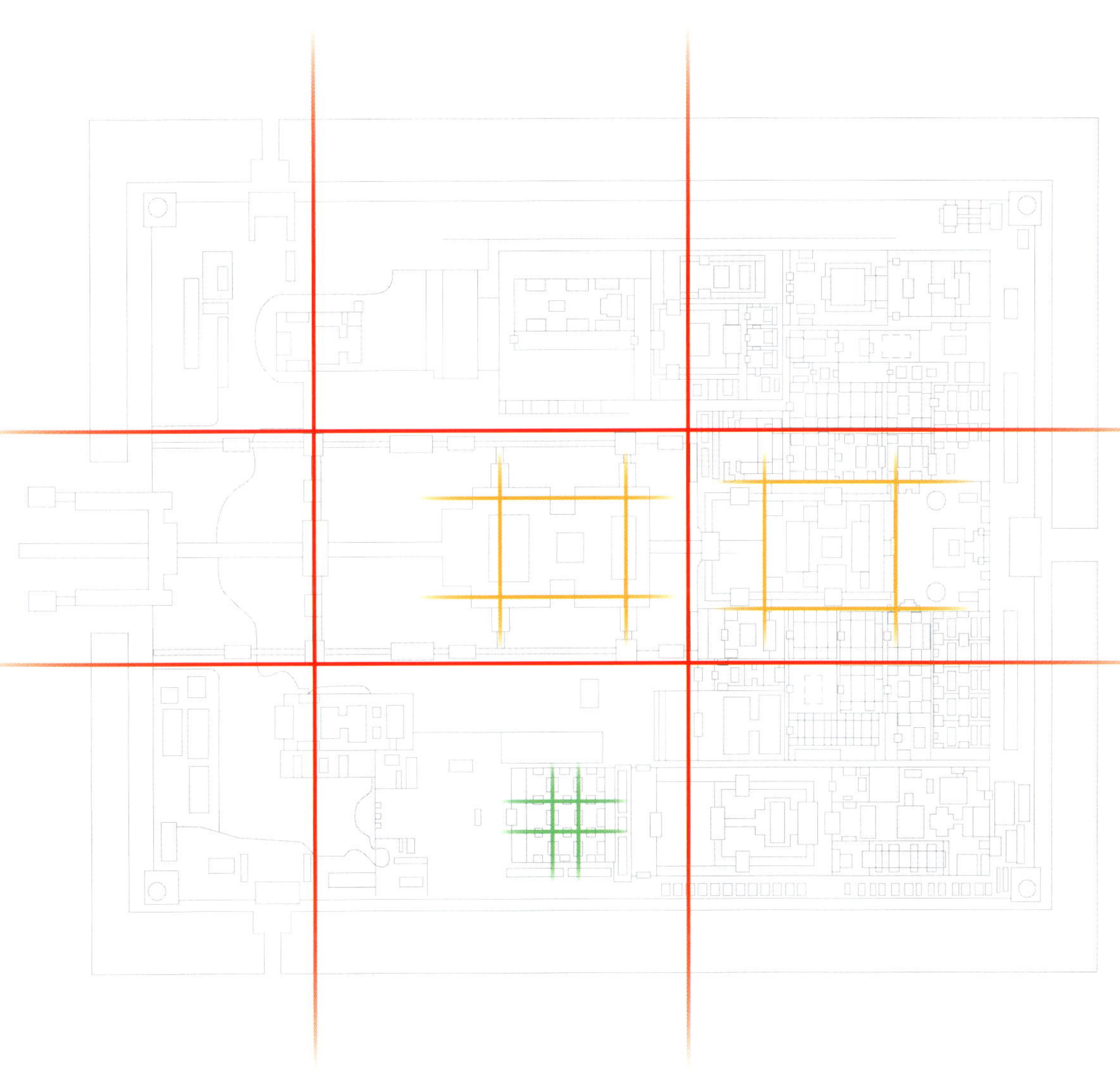

F IG 4.30 EDWARD HOPPER, NIGHTHAWKS

Hopper's subtle use of the nine-square pattern in "Nighthawks" is powerful and difficult to ignore once you discover it.

Taking the nine-square concept and applying it to some of our greatest works of art, we find some remarkable similarities between startlingly divergent styles.

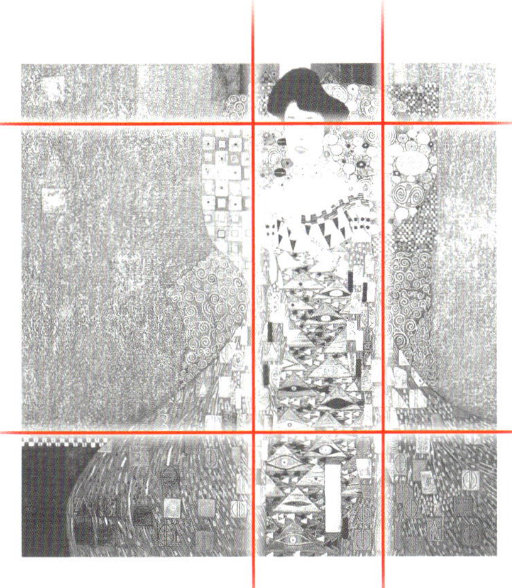

FIG. 4.31 GUSTAV KLIMT, THE WOMAN IN GOLD

Klimt's 1907 work is considered a seminal painting in the emergence of the modern art era. A beautiful portrait comprised of flat planes utilizing Byzantine art patterns, the nine-square composition enhances the balance of style and elegance.

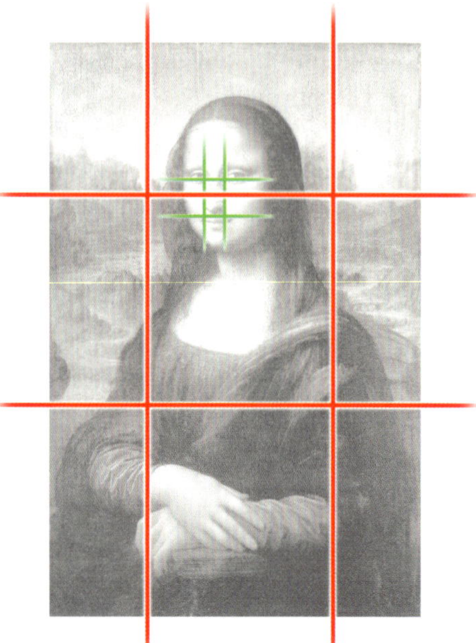

FIG 4.32 | LEONARDO DA VINCI, MONA LISA

The "Mona Lisa" by Leonardo da Vinci (1503) is probably the most famous painting in the world. The enigmatic beauty of the subject and the atmospheric quality of the background broke new ground for artists that led the way for the future.

Fig 4.33 | CLYFFORD STILL, untitled, 1957 Clyfford Still (1904-1980) was an American painter and one of the leading figures in the first generation of Abstract Expressionists. Utilizing Color Field theory, he created elegant and beautiful work in part by subtly utilizing a nine-square fractal patterning.

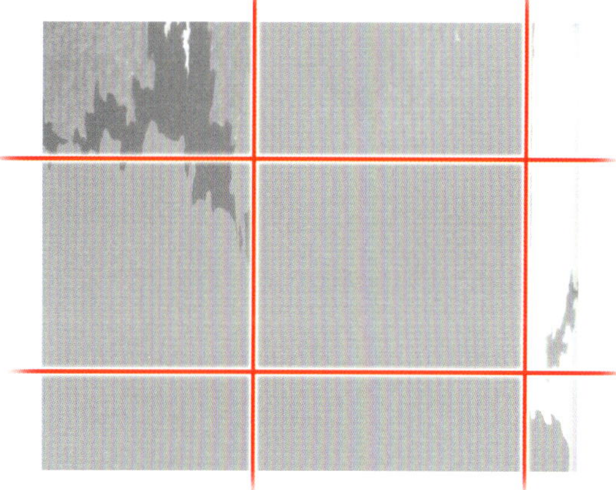

FIG. 4.34 | SANDRO BOTICELLI, BIRTH OF VENUS

The left vertical aligns between two faces on the top and a right-angled bend in the shell below. The right vertical aligns in a circular fold in the red cloth above and the red cloth below. The top horizontal aligns the horizon and Venus' navel. The lower horizontal aligns the left figure's toe with the right figure's knee (with accompanying response in her robe's folds).

As with the works of architecture presented and analyzed earlier in this chapter, these works of art all have the nine square as the root of their pattern. The artworks shown here are considered some of the most beautiful works known to humankind. These are works that are cherished, protected and admired as beautiful worldwide.

In the Introduction, I recounted two instances that related to people experiencing our work early in my career. The first was someone who experienced "beauty" when viewing our work. The second was someone who said our work was "interesting and unique."

We now know that the component that generated the emotion of beauty was the presence of the nine-square model in the home design. And the experience of "interesting and unique" was the absence of the nine-square model. It relates to the parasympathetic and sympathetic emotional responses outlined in Chapter 2. This, once again, is about the approach-avoidance response: pleasure or survival.

This overview of some of humanity's most beautiful and iconic works of architecture and art indicates that the utilization of the nine-square pattern is an important component of each of the works. As we will show in Chapter 6, we are born with an intuitive inclination to read patterns, and this one pattern and the deep pool of variations that have evolved from it are fundamental to understanding beauty. The emotion of beauty in this instance is a reaction to a pattern, and that pattern is the nine square.

GEOGRAPHICAL OVERVIEW

Nobody wishes to conserve a building if it does not look right; but if it does look right, someone will find a use for it.

ROGER SCRUTON

You don't have to know about mirror neurons to know
that certain patterns and shapes produce empathetic reactions in an observer.

JOHN P. EBERHARD

Architecture is our primary instrument in relating us with space and time, and giving these dimensions a human measure. It domesticates limitless space and endless time to be tolerated, inhabited and understood by humankind.

JUHANI PALLASMAA

PYRAMIDS OF MEROE, SUDAN

The Kushite kingdoms in the lower Nile Valley created these tombs between 300 B.C. and 300 A.D.

The path that has led us to this analysis was thousands of years in the making, encompassing multiple continents and civilizations. In Western society, architectural history generally begins with the Grecian period, with the most notable building being the Parthenon. The unique aspect of this building is that we will use that era as a recent example of the use of the nine-square pattern and go back 5,000 years.

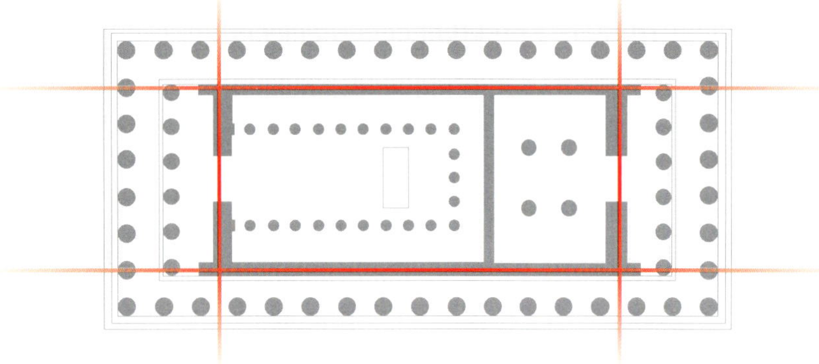

FIG 5.1 | THE PARTHENON

The Parthenon, considered the most important surviving building from classical Greece, was the zenith of the Doric Order. Begun in 447 B.C. and completed in 438 B.C., it was part of the Athenian Empire and is an enduring symbol of ancient Greece and Western civilization. As analyzed in Chapter 4, the Parthenon is a series of nine-square patterns overlaid onto one another. This deep sense of layering and ambiguity of the order creates a curiosity in the beholder, leading to the feeling of beauty.

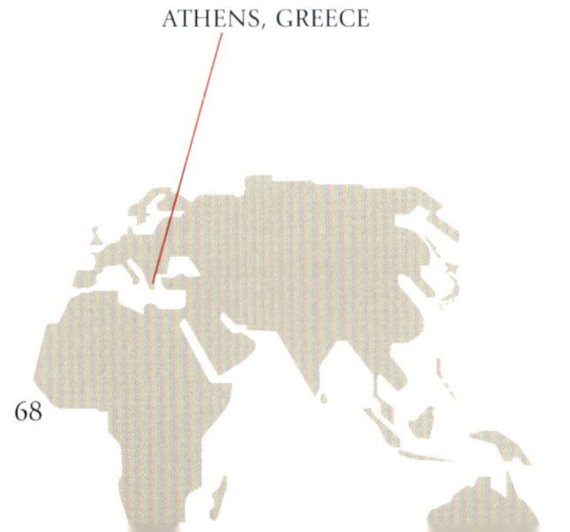

FIG. 5.2 | THE NECROMANTEION OF EPHYRA

Predating the Parthenon is the Necromanteion of Ephyra, which dates to 1300 B.C. The subterranean structure was comprised of six distinct chambers organized around a central corridor, a clear derivative of the nine-square pattern.

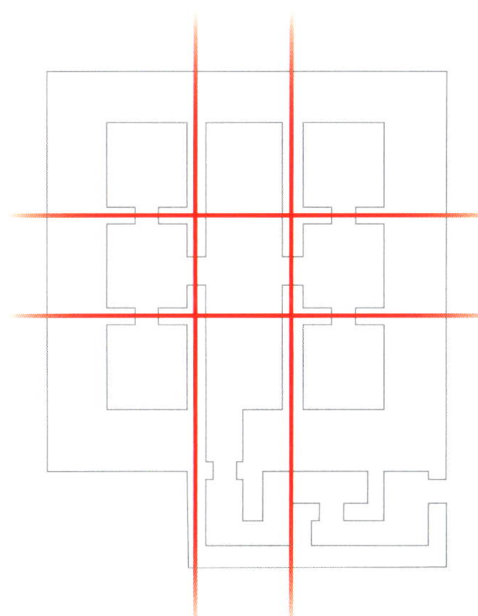

FIG 5.3 | CHICHEN ITZA, MEXICO

Mesoamerican civilizations developed in the pre-Columbian Americas beginning roughly in 1800 B.C. Today these civilizations are known for their architecture, mathematics and astronomy — especially their monumental architecture that focused on pyramid and temple construction. Chichen Itza is a product of the Terminal Classic period of Mayan culture (800–900 A.D.). These buildings, especially the ceremonial ones, used the nine-square pattern.

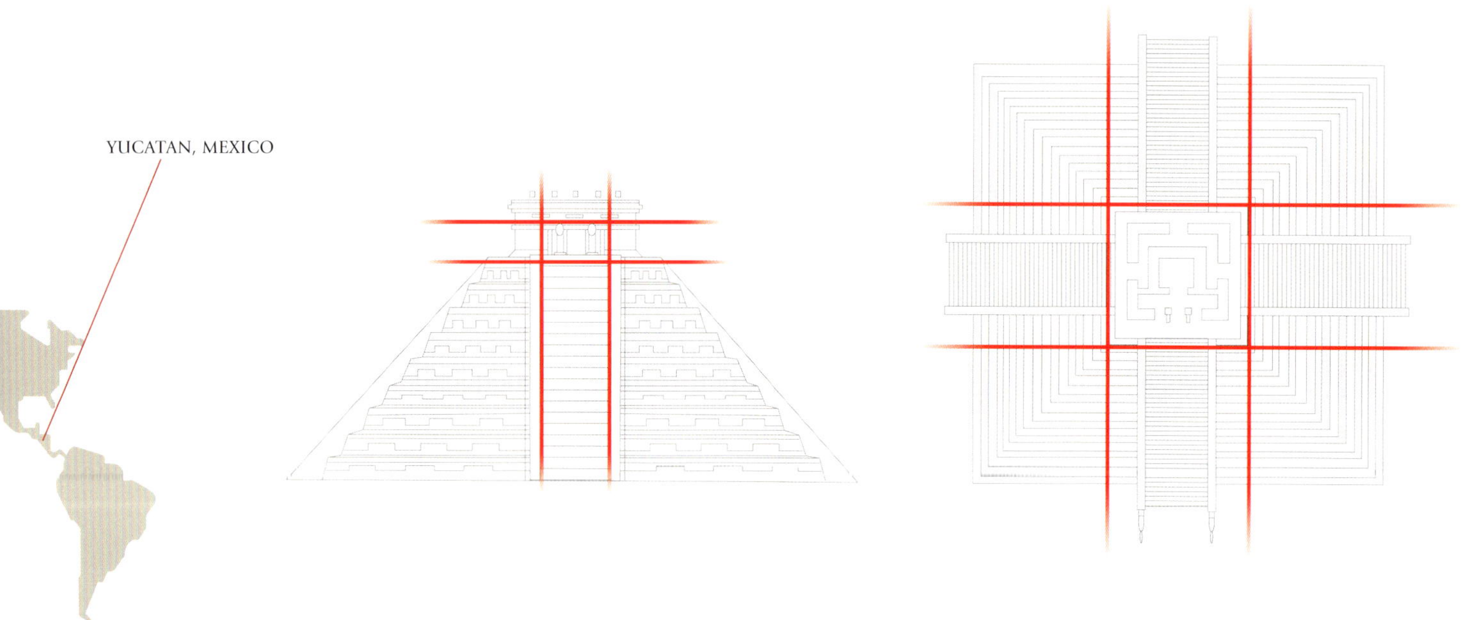

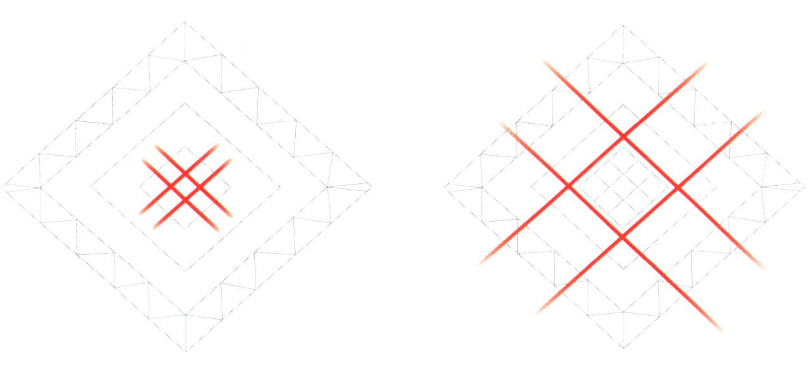

FIG. 5.4 | BUSH BARROW, STONEHENGE

In 1808 near Stonehenge, excavation at Bush Barrow unearthed remains known as the "King of Stonehenge" that date to 2000 B.C. Found attached to the remains of this body was a gold-bronze medallion that became known as the Bush Barrow Lozenge. This work of craftsmanship represents the nine-square pattern at the center of a square medallion representing authority, the sacred and the beautiful.

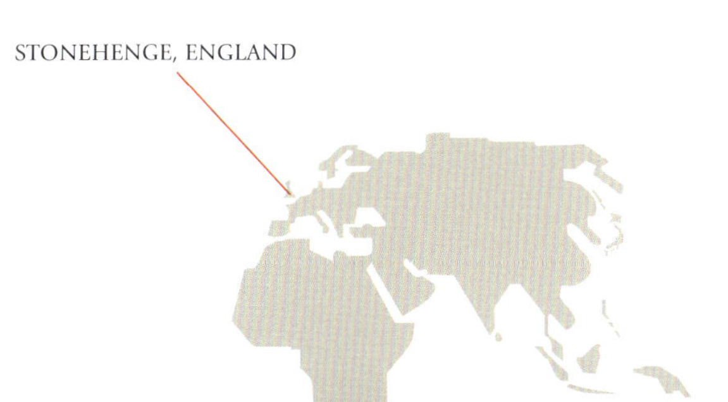

FIG. 5.5 | GIZA PYRAMID COMPLEX, EGYPT

Egyptian civilization built the great pyramid complex of Giza from 2560 B.C. to 2540 B.C. Comprised of three main pyramids — Khufu, Khafre and Menkaure, as well as the Sphinx and other contributing structures — the pyramids are the essence of ancient Egyptian beauty. The complex is one of the Seven Wonders of the World and the only one still in existence. The nine-square pattern overlays the individual pyramid plans, as well as the entire site plan.

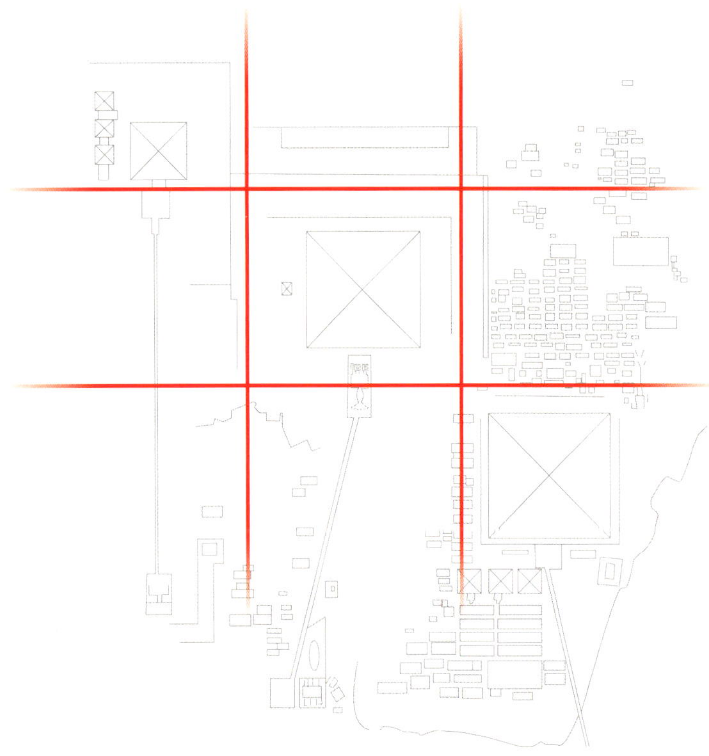

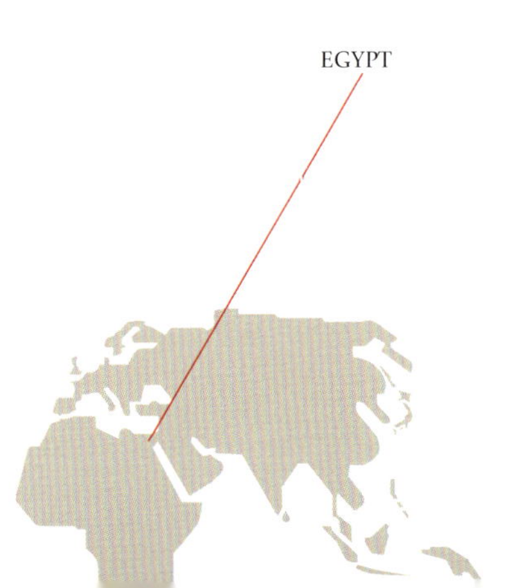

FIG. 5.6 | YANGSHAO GREAT HOUSE, CHINA

Chinese Yangshao culture thrived in 5000 B.C. during the Neolithic Period. Located in the town of Banpo near the Wei He River, the village plan and the Great House, which archeologists recently reconstructed, both display the advanced planning concepts utilized at that time. Based on the nine-square pattern, which had holy status in the culture (Alfred Schinz, *The Magic Square, Cities of Ancient China*, 1996), this is the earliest known manifestation of the utilization of this pattern. Following the Yangshuo, the Magic Square concept was used as a pattern for the layout of the royal city of Zhengzhou in 2000 B.C.

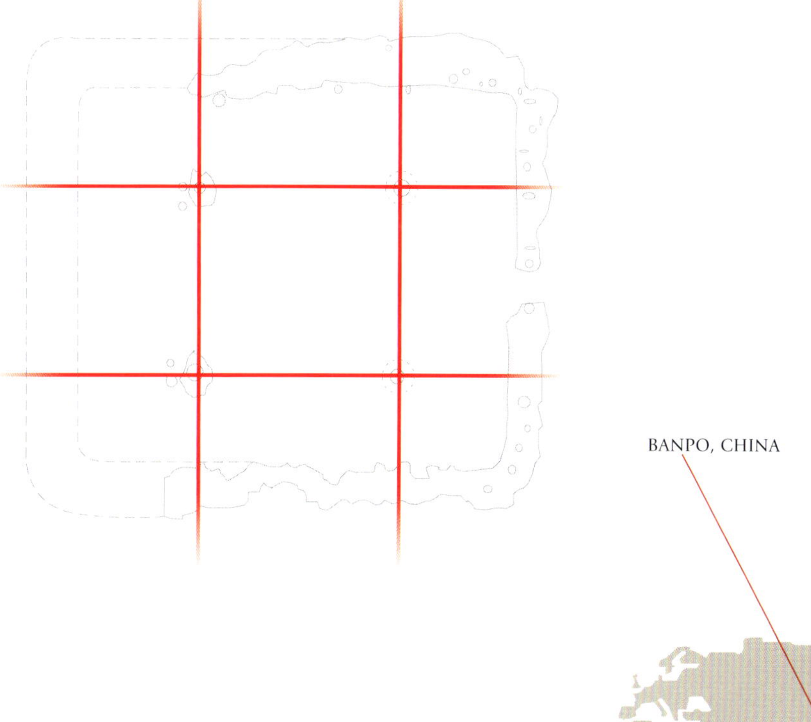

BANPO, CHINA

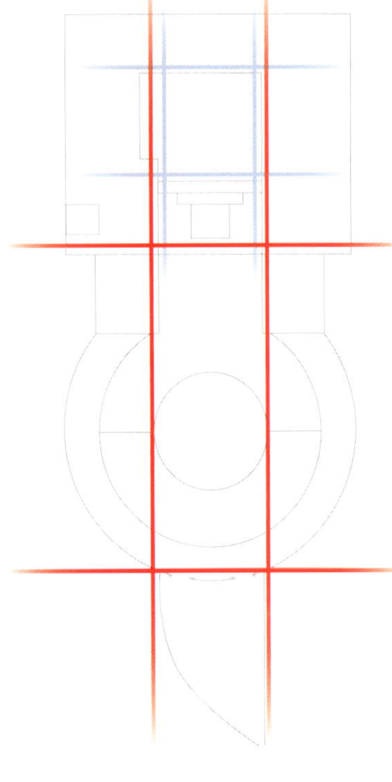

FIG 5.7 | CARAL PERU

Caral was inhabited roughly between the 26th and 20th centuries B.C., enclosing an area of more than 60 hectares (150 acres). Caral was described by its excavators as the oldest urban center in the Americas, a claim that was later challenged as other ancient sites were found nearby, such as Bandurria, Peru. Accommodating more than 3,000 inhabitants, it is the best-studied and one of the largest Norte Chico sites known.

PERU

These famous buildings are linked by the nine-square grid despite their scope of geographical locations and occurring centuries apart. This raises a question: With such extreme separation of time and space, how is the pattern still prevalent? Cross-cultural information sharing was unlikely to have spread the idea. Seemingly, the root of the pattern is founded on a universal truth common to all civilizations and has been for all time.

Anthropomorphic forms have long been an inspiration in architecture and art. The beauty, proportions, and rhythms that nature provides are bases of design. The nine square is one of the root patterns provided by nature, and it's a clear steppingstone to beauty that can be found even on the human face.

FIG 5.8 | BAULE MASK, GUINEA COAST, AFRICA

EMOTIONAL BONDING

The longer I live the more beautiful life becomes. If you foolishly ignore beauty, you will soon find yourself without it. Your life will be impoverished. But if you invest in beauty, it will remain with you all the days of your life.

FRANK LLOYD WRIGHT

You employ stone, wood and concrete, and with these materials you build houses and palaces. That is construction. Ingenuity is at work. But suddenly you touch my heart, you do me good, I am happy and I say: This is beautiful. That is Architecture. Art enters in.

LE CORBUSIER

The Three Levels of Acquiring Intelligence:
Information, Knowledge, Wisdom

JUHANI PALLASMAA

Newborns come into the world with sensitivities and capacities that predispose them to join in emotional communion with others. These same sensitivities and capacities are later used and elaborated in the rhythms and modes of adult love, art and architecture.

ELLEN DISSANAYAKE, *ART AND INTIMACY: HOW THE ARTS BEGAN*

There is a famous story about a Scottish medical scientist who in 1928 returned from a month-long holiday to his lab to find that his petri dishes were infected with a green mold despite being carefully stored. Upon looking more closely under the microscope, he realized that the green mold had completely killed the bacterial cultures he had been studiously preparing.

How could that happen? The green mold wasn't anything new or unknown to lab technicians, as it had nullified many experiments over the years. What was especially different this time was the degree to which the mold had neutralized the bacteria. He wondered how this might affect treatment procedures if doctors had such a tool at their disposal.

RONDA, SPAIN

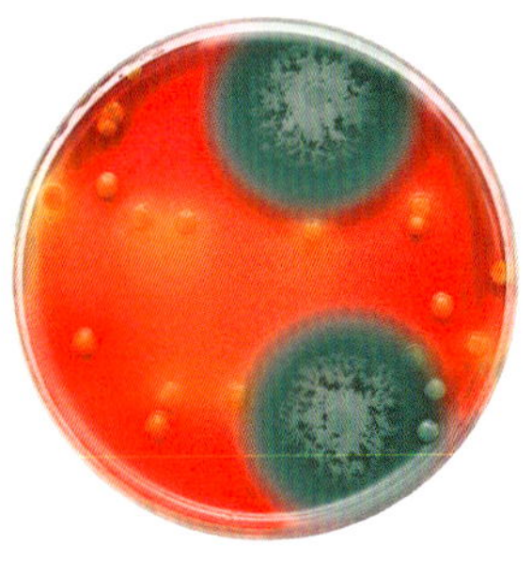

FIG.6.1 | GREEN MOLD

A problem may hold a lesson.

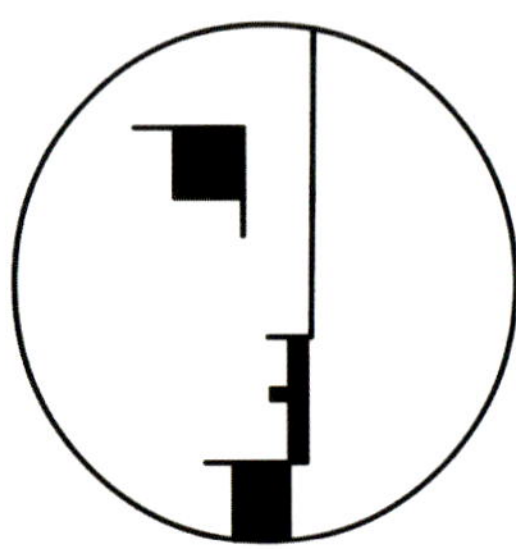

FIG.6.2 | BAUHAUS LOGO

The pattern lurks within.

FIG.6.3 | AMERICA, HIRAM POWERS

Fast forward 10 years and after much work by a vast team of scientists, penicillin was introduced to the world as the first anti-bacterial treatment. By recognizing that something seen as a negative had possible broader positive implications, Dr. Alexander Fleming changed the course of human history. He and two colleagues were awarded the Nobel Prize for his work in 1945.

This story inspires me to look beyond conventional wisdom and expectations to ask, "What if?"

When beauty fell out of favor

When Walter Gropius, along with several other individuals, initiated the Bauhaus school in Weimar, Germany, in 1919, he did so with the clear intent of fomenting a revolution in thought and craft of art and architecture. As detailed in Chapter 1, European society at that time was under extreme pressure to rebuild from WWI. New, more efficient methods of construction and design that eliminated time-consuming details were created to aid in the recovery. Time-consuming details and construction methods were deemed superfluous and unnecessary.

And thus was born the anti-beauty culture of architecture. Beauty was being redefined as functional, spare and structural. Aspects that appealed to the human soul were deemed irrelevant and not to be held in high esteem.

Architecture had long utilized nature and the human form to create forms, details and proportions. But Bauhaus teachings declared those ideals to be no longer valid, thus neutralizing thousands of years of thought and wisdom born of continual experimentation.

Early in my education, we were instructed to avoid patterns that had humanistic overtones, for fear of not being honest — not truly born of function but rather, contrived as *a priori* ideas that improperly influenced the proper course of the design. True design, we were instructed, came only from functional analysis. To quote Gropius: "A modern building should derive its architectural significance solely from the vigor and consequence of its own organic proportions. It must be true to itself, logically transparent and virginal of lies or trivialities."

Peter Behrens, who taught Gropius and set him on his path, was even more strident: "Design is not about decorating functional forms — it is about creating forms that accord with the character of the object and that show new technologies to advantage."

From the mouths of babes

One event had important implications in my evolution as an architect, and it bears some semblance to the penicillin story. I was presenting some drawings, which included rendered elevations, to a client. It was a typical design meeting, where items were discussed and the client commented about the design. The word "beautiful" even was used to describe certain aspects of the idea. The clients were warming up to the ideas.

Their 5-year-old daughter was watching and I remember thinking how captivated she seemed to be, especially by the elevation that was propped up against the wall on a display board. Finally, she walked over, looked more closely and exclaimed, "It's a face."

I was concerned, of course, because the modernist lessons of avoiding anthropomorphic forms at all costs still resonated with me. Yet she had caught her parents' attention, and they discussed the pattern in the elevation that resembled a face. I didn't see it at first, but as the discussion carried on, it became evident to me.

In the following days, I couldn't keep the comment, "It's a face" from repeating in my mind. This was important in that the clients loved the elevation, and I was reluctant to change the pattern. Yet, what was I to do about not being honest and true to the design process when I intuitively had landed on a facial pattern to compose the elevation?

I, too, was blessed with young children in my home at this period of my life. Our refrigerator door had a great collection of children's art. In the center of the collection was a home that one of my children had drawn. If you ask a child to draw a house, it generally has a recognizable pattern: two windows up high and two windows low with a door in the center — five elements arranged symmetrically left to right. This is exactly what was on my refrigerator. This, in fact, was the pattern imbedded in the elevation, the one declared "a face" by my client's child.

I had clients request a Georgian-style design. In doing research on the style, there was a startling realization. If you look closely at a typical Georgian house in its most simple form, the same pattern applies: A facial pattern was imbedded in one of the greatest design schemes ever developed. It could hardly be any more evident. I also knew that the Georgian style was rooted in Palladianism, which is rooted in the nine-square design. Could there somehow be a link between beauty, facial patterning and the nine square?

FIG.6.4 | BOTTOM-UP DRAWING

Children intuitively draw houses with a face pattern.

FIG. 6.5

A Georgian house designed by Ruggles Mabe Studio, exhibiting the nine-square pattern.

The penicillin story floated out of my subconscious, jolting me to ask: Could what we had been taught in our modernist education be incorrect? Should we be looking in the opposite direction and embracing humanistic forms in architecture? There seemed to be some important forces at work here. Could it be that beauty recognition, history and intuition all emanated from this pattern? This initiated my slow and steady investigation of looking into facial patterns, nine-square patterns and their application to beauty.

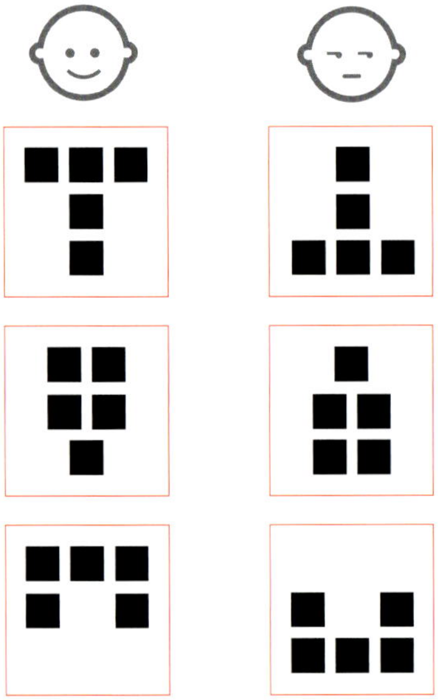

FIG. 6.6

Babies prefer the top-heavy, facial-hinting patterns on the left.

Some of my discoveries

■ Research has shown that there is a facial pattern that infants prefer (fig. 6.6). This pattern bears a remarkable resemblance to a nine-square pattern. The hypothesis here is that the nine-square pattern was intuitively developed over thousands of years as a result of the facial pattern-recognition skill that all humans are born with. This geometric pattern is a representation of a parent's face, and the face represents the empathic bonding that happens between parent and child: pleasure and love.

■ At birth, 65 percent of the neuronal structure of our brain is dedicated to facial recognition. Over half of our structural mental capacity is given to facial-pattern recognition. Why, in our evolution, would nature devote so much capacity to this skill?

"Faces are among the most informative stimuli we ever perceive: Even a split-second glimpse of a person's face tells us their identity, sex, mood, age, race and direction of attention." (*Tsao and Livingstone, Age of Insight: The Quest to Un-*

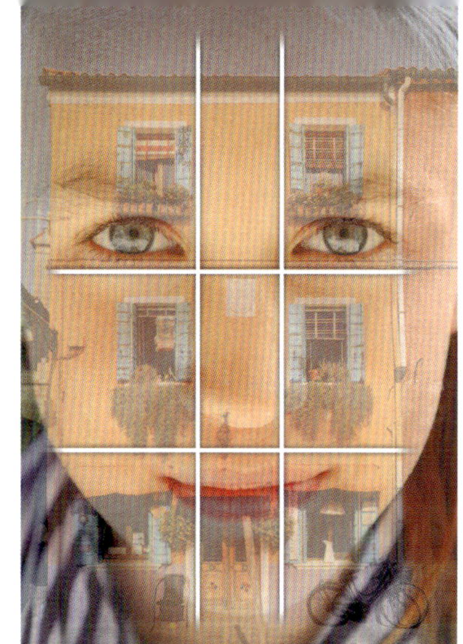
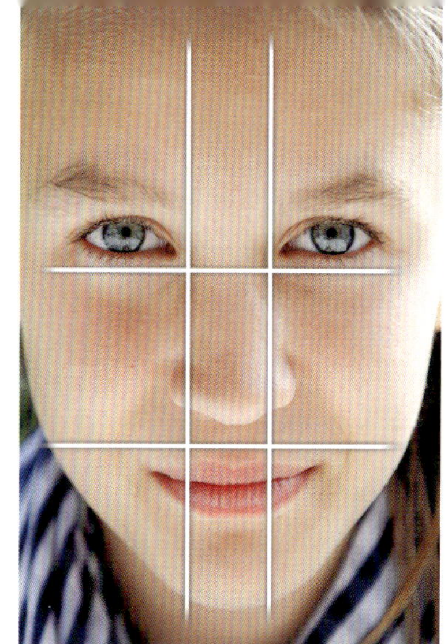

FIG. 6.7

The four divisions and the "nine-square" — a primal pattern

derstand the Unconscious in Art, Mind, and Brain from Vienna 1900 to the Present, 2012, page 287).

Psychology Professor David Perrett writes in *In Your Face, The New Science of Human Attraction,* (2010), "Our constant, intense, and rewarding exposure to faces means that faces acquire a prominence and a significance for us that no other object can match."

■ The brain mechanisms underlying face recognition emerge early in infancy (Kandel, *Age of Insight,* page 288). Babies prefer to look at faces from the first moments of birth. It is, as Darwin theorized, part of the survival instinct that humans are born with. Darwin pointed out that if infants are to survive, they need adults to respond to and care for them.

In a groundbreaking study, John Morton and Mark H. Johnson of the Medical Research Council, Cognitive Development Unit in London, England, theorized that "infants possess some information about the structural characteristics of faces from birth."

This theory follows from research of Robert Fantz, who argued: that, "It is ... reasonable to suppose that the early interest of infants in form and pattern in general, as well as in particular kinds of pattern, play an important role in the development of behavior by focusing attention on stimuli that will later have adaptive significance" (Fantz, Robert, "The Origin of Form Perception," *Scientific American*, Issue 204, page 66-72, 1961). Following additional research, Morton and Johnson wrote, "At normal viewing distance a 1-month-old infant can at best discern only the grossest features of the face: the outer contour defined by the hairline and vague darker areas in the regions of the eyes and mouth."

"From birth, babies can feel pleasure, distress and even fear. By the time they've reached two years of age they have developed some pretty complex emotions," according to author Lauren's Barack's 2016 article in *Parenting Magazine* titled "How Babies Learn About Feelings,"

One of those complex emotions is empathy, associated with the bonding that takes place between parent and child beginning from the first moments of birth. Love, nurturing, survival, protection and sustenance are all part of the bonding. The child quickly knows that their survival needs can be met, and there is a feeling of empathy.

FIG. 6.8 | THE INFANT'S VIEW

An infant can discern those feelings from someone's face. Nature has given the newborn the ability to discern facial features at the distance from the child's face to the mother's face during nursing, which signifies survival and pleasure. The facial pattern represents the emotions of love, nurturing and survival. Those emotions initiate the emotion of empathy and feelings of pleasure.

FIG. 6.9 | A FACE TO APPROACH

In *Newborns' Preference for Faces: What is Crucial*, by Chiara Turati, Francesca Simion, Idanna Milani and Carlo Umilta, University of Padua (2002), they write that "the meaningful experience newborn infants have with human faces drives the perceptual preference for stimuli that share similar qualities. Similar patterns to the face share and engender similar emotional responses."

The facial pattern recognition beginning from birth elicits a response of love, nurturing, survival, protection and empathy, the general sense of bonding. This bonding generates neuronal pathways in our brain that last a lifetime, ready to be activated upon viewing a facial pattern. Children are born with a drive to explore. A quality of exploring is curiosity, which in turn is the initial component in the three-step theory of beauty outlined in Chapter 2 (page 14).

■ Of course, there are degrees to this perception, and the push-pull of pattern recognition is in play here. Opposing systems push against each other to reach a balance point, which is adjustable (*The Happiness Hypothesis: Finding Modern Truth in Ancient Wisdom*, by Jonathan Haidt, 2006). We are constantly assessing if a pattern is about approach or avoidance and to what degree. So should we encounter a facial pattern that has threatening qualities, then the avoidance reaction may come into play.

FIG. 6.10 | A FACE TO AVOID

Neonatal bonding recall is a positive experience triggered by facial pattern

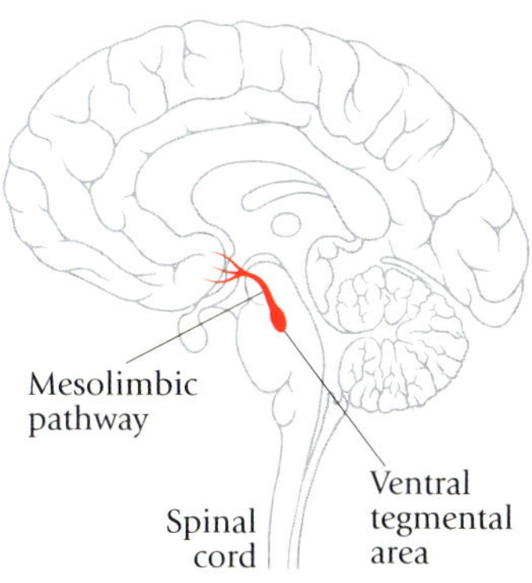

FIG. 6.11 | BONDING

The Mesolimbic (reward) Pathway regulates motivation and desire for rewarding stimuli, generating endorphins and, with positive stimuli, pleasure. Facial pattern recognition uses this feedback system in the process we call bonding.

recognition. Theoretically, despite the stronger neurological reaction being the avoidance instinct, the recurrence of love and nurturing is the longer-lasting, more-affirmative quality that humans seek. Pleasure wins out, in the long run, over avoidance.

■ Hermann von Helmholtz, a noted 19th-century physician, postulated that the push-pull of pattern recognition is governed by "bottom-up" information and "top-down information."

Top-down refers to cognitive influences and higher-order mental functions such as expectations, attention, imagery and learned visual associations. Essentially, the brain accesses acquired information to discern what emotion is being felt. This type of processing resolves ambiguities in patterns in the field of vision. If the brain vaguely recognizes a pattern, then this cognitive process will help complete the pattern.

Bottom-up processing is based on circuitry that is inherent in our brain. It is

TOP-DOWN PROCESSING

Have I seen this before?

Formulate hypothesis on nature of a stimulus as a whole system

Utilize known models, ideas, and expectations to interpret sensory information

Recognize and categorize stimulus with other known information

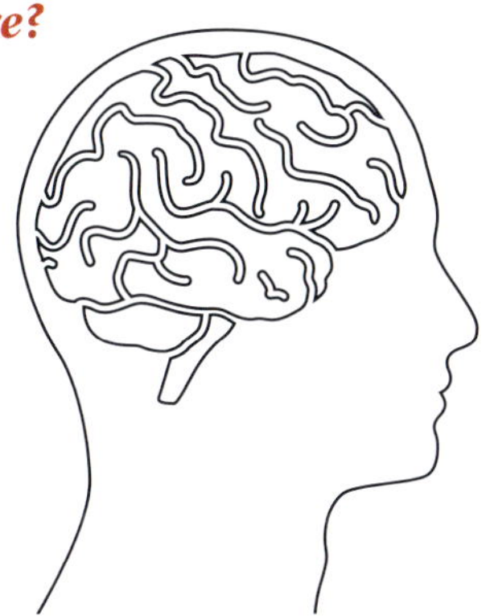

Recognize stimulus and integrate it into bigger picture

Combine specific features of stimulus into more complex forms

Analyze specific sensory information about stimulus

What am I seeing?

BOTTOM-UP PROCESSING

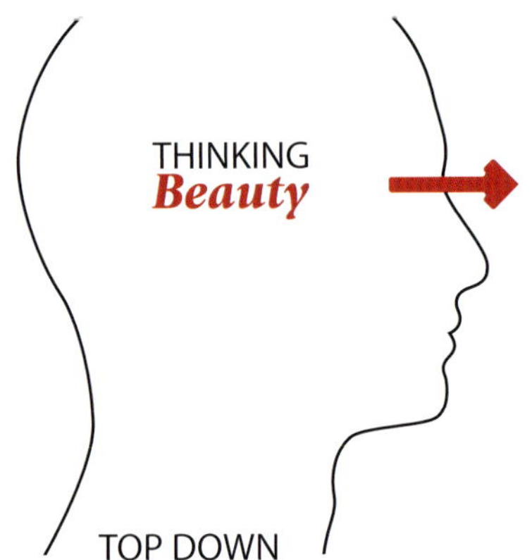

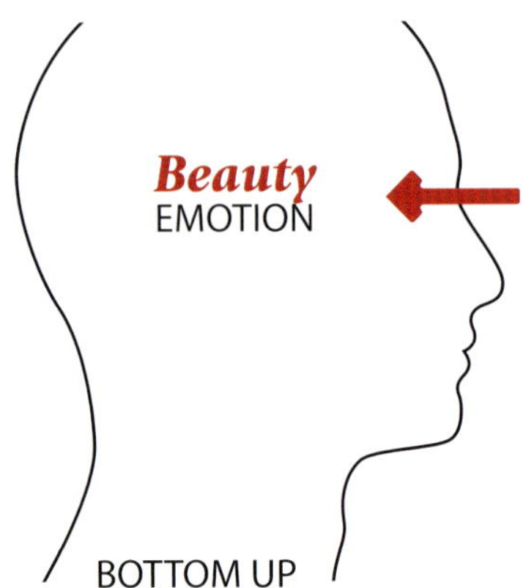

FIG. 6.12 | BEAUTY

Top-down projects thought during perception.

Bottom-up generates emotion immediately via the autonomic nervous system.

essentially innate, intuitive knowledge that initiates the emotion. The processing is governed by universal rules that are built into the brain at birth by biological evolution, and it enables us to extract key elements of images and patterns in the physical world, including intersections, contours and crossing of lines. So, the push-pull isn't just between approach or avoidance; it is also about intuition and cognition.

This is an important point because a newborn child possesses minimal accumulated information, therefore the intuitive, born-with emotions govern their actions. Bottom-up processing wins out and the innate drive for pleasure and food becomes the determining factors that foster bonding.

■ The nine-square pattern has a worldwide history that spans thousands of years. How could that be? This hypothesis allows an explanation: Parental bonding is part of all human existence, and the pattern is constant throughout time and space, and has been for all time.

As quoted in Chapter 2, Professor Harry Francis Mallgrave stated, "Beauty is a neurological activity, an urge for and feeling of pleasure emanating from the brain's lowest or most primal reaches and associated with awe or wonder." He also said, "In this regard, we judge certain forms to be beautiful because they in fact mirror the basic conditions of organic life."

The famous Scottish philosopher David Hume said, "Beauty is no quality in things themselves. It exists merely in the mind, which contemplates them; and each mind perceives a different beauty." From this originates the common refrain, "Beauty is in the eye of the beholder," which is a top-down statement.

Let us use the penicillin story as a model and reverse the thinking here. Beauty is an emotion common to us all that creates a feeling that results in an interpretation. Beauty is a bottom-up emotion and not a top-down processing of accumulated information.

Hume seems to recognize this as well in another quote: "Beauty, whether moral or natural, is felt more properly than perceived." The emotion of beauty exists in us all, and our feelings towards beauty are tempered by societal expectations and customs in top-down processing.

■ Bilateral symmetry is an important component in facial-pattern recognition as related to beauty. The anthropologist Karl Grammar, working with biologist Randy Thornhill, measured facial symmetry by measuring distances from facial landmarks and found that symmetry correlated with judgments of attractiveness. This has been confirmed with many subsequent studies and experiments. Facial symmetry equates with beauty.

One theory holds that symmetry conveys the image of health and that good genes are present. This is representative of being an attractive mate with whom to conceive children. Symmetry is a fitness indicator that reflects a healthy nervous system, a healthy immune system. This holds true for infants and adults as well as people from different cultures. Beauty seems to have constants that cut across ages and racial boundaries (*The Aesthetic Brain*, page 15) as the principles of attraction in faces have a biological and evolutionary foundation.

Symmetry conveys a sense of health, well-being and solidity. In the architectural sense, as shown in Chapter 4 and the analysis of iconic art and architectural works worldwide, symmetry plays a major part in the anointment of a work as a timeless and iconic beauty. I believe the less symmetrical, the less likely for the composition to be judged beautiful.

In 2000, Christopher Tyler presented the paper, "The Human Expression of Symmetry" at the International Conference on the Unity of the Sciences in Seoul, Korea. There he stated that, "Symmetry is an important visual property for humans because it can be useful in discriminating living organisms from inanimate objects." He also suggested that humans see symmetry as an important principle in objects we design, from buildings to Persian rugs.

According to John Eberhard in *Brain Landscape* (2009), humans can detect symmetry within about 0.05 of a second. This stimulus duration is too brief for eye movements to be completed. This implies that human symmetry processing is a global, hard-wired activity of the brain.

Since antiquity, architectural proportioning systems have been important, and many studies have been made looking for the geometric properties of facial structure in an attempt to define beauty. This is especially true with use of the Golden Ratio of 1.618 and the Golden Section, which is a graphic depiction of the Golden Ratio. What is important to realize here is that most of these studies were made prior to the understanding that neuroscience has provided us with hormonal reaction to patterns. The Golden Ratio and the Golden Section are recurring themes in beauty, especially in fractals and repetitively coded geometry. We intrinsically react to these proportions because our evolution tells us that the

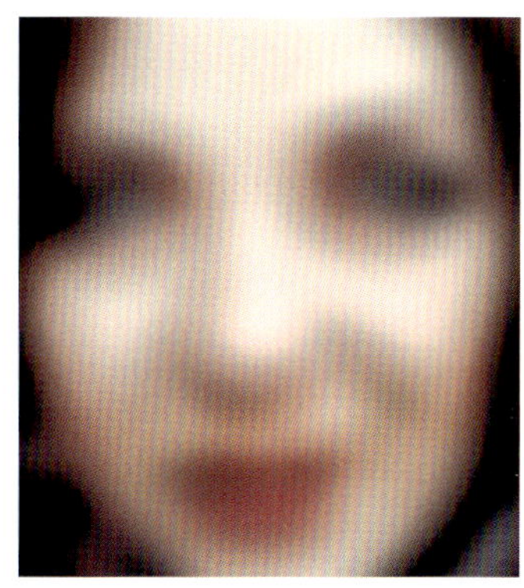

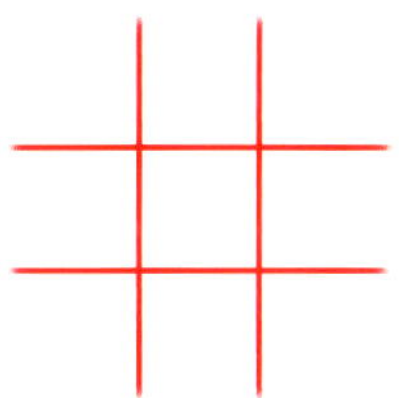

FIG. 6.13 | A PERSISTENT ABSTRACTION FROM OUR INFANCY

The nine-square pattern imprints the infant mind and returns again and again in our cultural artifacts.

patterns will support our survival and/or pleasure. Our acknowledgment of the code and pattern is ingrained in our DNA.

The singular message here is that the three-by-three pattern known as the nine square results in triggering the sequence of curiosity, reward and pleasure that activates the hormonal system, which results in the feeling of pleasure and the acknowledgment of beauty. While proportions are important, without the presence of one of the fundamental patterns, curiosity is not initiated and the sequence is interrupted. Should the lack of the fundamental pattern be replaced by an unfamiliar pattern that generates high stress in the observer, then the reaction is likely to be a sympathetic, adrenalized reaction that activates the fight-or-flight reaction for survival and avoidance.

In psychology, there is a phenomenon referred to as Pareidolia, in which a vague, random stimulus is perceived as significant. According to Hume, "There is a universal tendency among mankind to conceive all beings like themselves, and to transfer to every object those qualities with which they are familiarly acquainted and of which they are intimately conscious."

Transferring the emotions of beauty into a building elevation upon viewing the nine-square pattern is an empathic reaction that results in pleasure. Through the millennia of evolution, parental love and bonding have imprinted our neuronal structure to look for, uncover and acknowledge the nine-square pattern.

When self-referring geometric systems known as fractals are present, then the response is an even stronger emotional and empathic response, one that generates a self-referring sense of curiosity and pleasure that feels insatiable. This is the feeling one has in the presence of the Mona Lisa, sitting in Radcliffe Square in Oxford, viewing the Monet lily paintings or standing outside Fallingwater. This is what our iconic works of art and architecture are made of.

Our brains have powerful machinery for processing scenes, objects and particularly faces. The associative recall of the bonding emotion and the transference of the feeling to a work of architecture or art via the nine-square pattern makes this an inherently pleasurable experience.

My research shows it is pleasurable because it stimulates our brains to initiate the hedonic outflow pathways of our neuronal structure, releasing the hormone endorphin. These pathways are the result of empathic love that occurs during neonatal bonding. This feeling of pleasure results in the top-down proclamation, "It's beautiful." It is a bottom-up emotion ignited by the single ancient pattern that man has known for all time: a geometric representation of our facial pattern, the nine square.

In summary, beauty is a physical reaction to a pattern that conveys the emotion of pleasure. Pleasure that is generated by this simple geometric scheme is one of the fundamental keys in the theory of beauty. What wisdom can we nurture from this knowledge and why is it important to humanity?

7 | INFORMED BY SCIENCE

FROM KNOWLEDGE TO WISDOM

Beauty is the apprehension of that which pleases.

ARISTOTLE (THOMAS AQUINAS TRANSLATION)

Beauty is not the source of disinterested pleasure, but simply the object of a universal interest: the interest that we have in beauty, and in the pleasure that beauty brings.

ROGER SCRUTON

We are an integral part of the world that we perceive; we are not external observers. We are situated within it. Our view of it is from within its midst. We are made up of the same atoms and the same light signals as are exchanged between pine trees in the mountains and stars in the galaxies.

CARLO ROVELLI, *SEVEN BRIEF LESSONS ON PHYSICS*

Beauty is a light in the heart.

KHALIL GIBRAN

Bold, sweeping arcs formed by a majestic hawk cut across the blue Colorado sky. Such beauty! It's early one spring morning and I walked up a cobbled driveway leading to a home that we recently had finished to meet a photographer. He was at the home on assignment for a national publication that was interested in publishing something about the house.

Suddenly, to my surprise, the owners walked out the front door. I was surprised because they had told me they would be out of town on vacation during the photography session. I asked what had brought them back home early and hoped it wasn't something urgent. No, the wife replied. "We decided our new home felt better than where we were vacationing. We grabbed the first plane we could because we couldn't wait to be back here!" She added that she and her husband felt like

FIG. 7.1 | TWO DESIGN PATHWAYS

The Royal Ontario Museum in Toronto, designed by Daniel Libeskind, shows an interesting juxtaposition of two design styles. The new addition on the right is very strong on excitement and stimulation, elements of the autonomic nervous system's ***sympathetic*** inputs. The original museum building's architecture draws on ***parasympathetic*** forms, a quieter, more comforting approach.

they had received "so much more than we expected" in their new home. Each day, it feels joyful to wake up and experience something "beautiful," she said.

This sentiment was so telling. First, the expression, "We received so much more than we expected" has nothing to do with square footage, amenities or the home's cost. Additionally, the word "feels" in the statement was important, too, as it is an intuitive acknowledgment of an emotional reaction. This all relates to the intangible feeling of pleasure that the owners experience when in their home. It is subtle and insatiable. And importantly, as we will see, the feeling of pleasure is good for your health and sense of well-being because pleasure is stress-relieving.

Stress in society is at an epidemic level. High blood pressure, heart disease, stroke and cancer are all connected to stress. Cardiovascular disease caused by stress is the leading cause of death in the U.S. at a rate of more than seven times over other causes. Hypertension affects over 50 million people in the U.S. alone. All of this contributes to a chronic downward pull on our health, including the most fundamental foundation of human life, our DNA.

Psychology professors Elissa Epel and Elizabeth Blackburn at the University of California, San Francisco, in *The Telomere Effect* (2017), have measured the effects

of stress on repeating DNA at the end of chromosomes, called telomeres. When telomeres become too short (the result of stress), cells malfunction and lose their ability to divide, thus tissue no longer can renew itself.

FIG. 7.2 | TWO DESIGN PATHWAYS

The new Port House in Antwerp repurposes and renovates an old building into a new headquarters for the port. The addition and its ***sympathetic*** design forms dominate the original building's mostly ***parasympathetic*** forms. Zaha Hadid designed the new building.

We are talking about the very essence of the aging process. Stress doesn't just make us tired or ill; it also accelerates aging. Mary Armanios of Johns Hopkins School of Medicine in Baltimore, Maryland, advanced the research even further when she said, "Ten years on, there's no question in my mind that the environment has consequence on telomere length." It turns out that even our DNA, the most elemental of all components of life, is subject to ramifications from stress.

Living with chronic stress, even at low levels, leads to excessive stimulation of the sympathetic nervous system. This leads to prolonged periods where our biological repair functions are turned off, cellular aging accelerates and the ability of our DNA to reproduce is diminished. This is a slow, progressive, downward spiral. Eventually, a major breakdown occurs, perhaps a heart attack or any number of other degenerative complications.

Fortunately, for every action there is an opposite and equal reaction. The opposite reaction in this case would be the relaxation response orchestrated by a parasympathetic reaction. This reaction leads to the release of endorphins gen-

FIG. 7.3 | TWO DESIGN PATHWAYS

A ***sympathetic*** design supercedes a ***parasympathetic*** one at the Sharp Centre for Design, OCAD University, Toronto.

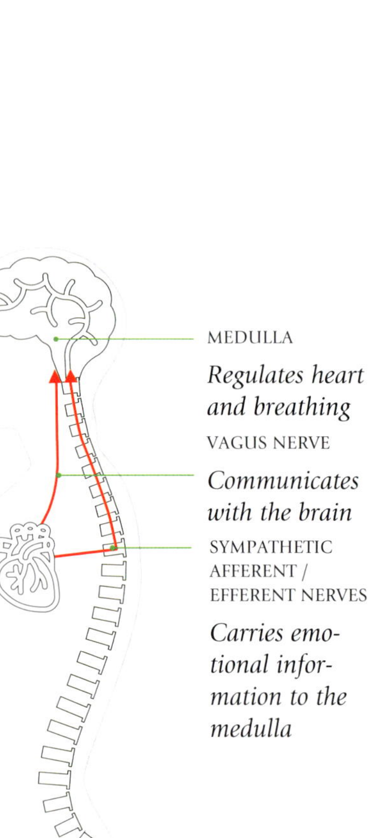

FIG. 7.4 | AUTONOMIC NERVOUS SYSTEM PATHWAYS

erating the feelings of pleasure, love and compassion. This is often when the emotion of beauty is activated. This response tempers and mediates a high-stress sympathetic reaction, and is known as the pleasure mode. As shown earlier in this work, the emotion of beauty is one of the initiators of the feeling of pleasure.

Jo Marchant in *Cure: A Journey Into the Science of Mind and Body* (2016), said, "(when a person) feels cared for and secure, rather than under threat, this alone can trigger significant biological changes that ease our (high stress) symptoms."

Patricia S. Churchland, in *Braintrust: What Neuroscience Tells Us about Morality* (2011), states, "Brains are organized to seek well-being, and to seek relief from ill-being. Thus, in a perfectly straightforward way, the circuitry for self-maintenance and the avoidance of pain is the source of the most basic values — the values of being alive and of well-being." As detailed previously, two of our basic, born-with inclinations are to seek pleasure and to avoid stress.

Perhaps by thinking about stress through the lens of our autonomic nervous system as an adrenalized sympathetic reaction, then we might say that society today exhibits all the symptoms of excessive sympathetic stimulation. Art and architecure play a critical role in this.

Of great importance, our living environment plays a key role in whether we are in pleasure or stress mode. In modern societies, many of us spend more than 80 percent of our time indoors and for most of us, the majority of our life is spent

FIG. 7.5 | BALANCED DESIGN

Robert A.M. Stern Architects designed the George W. Bush Presidential Center in Dallas, Texas. The orderly nine-square form of this building brings the comforts of the ***parasymathetic*** and at the same time projects a stimulating, ***sympathetic*** sense of grandeur and power.

engaged with architecture and art in some manner. This leaves a tremendous responsibility and opportunity on the doorstep of art and architecture.

Fortunately, we now have the science and the knowledge to eliminate some of this stress. Ellen Dissanayake in *Art and Intimacy: How the Arts Began* (2000), states, "Most people hunger for a more profound life. The arts (and architecture) are a way of treating the inner life seriously. They become embodiments of our affective experience. They put us in touch with our better self, allowing 'outcrops of transcendence.'"

One way of allowing for outcrops of transcendence would be to reduce the levels of chronic, low-level stress in our built environment with the utilization of the patterns that evolved from the savanna and matured through thousands of years of accumulated aesthetic wisdom: natural fractals and the nine-square pattern. At the same time, we should diminish the utilization of stress-inducing patterns and forms.

Our observations about the ancient brain have shown us that beauty in architecture and art are important to our sense of well-being. By bringing together the faculties of neuroscience, biology, psychology and architecture to create the new discipline of neuro-architectology, we can start to conceptualize our built environment to make us healthier and to improve our sense of well-being.

How we do this is an important area for further study. The good news is cur-

FIG. 7.6 | BALANCED DESIGN

The Thorncrown Chapel, designed by E. Fay Jones, sits in the forest in Eureka Springs, Arkansas. It utilizes the nine-square pattern with fractal scaling. The design balances the stimulation (***sympathetic***) of its verticality, transparency and 45° forms with the stability and calm of its ***parasymathetic*** nine-square form.

FIG. 7.7 | BALANCED DESIGN

National Gallery of Art, East Building, by I.M. Pei

rent technological capabilities offer hope. One example on the biology front is that scientists are now able to monitor the state of our autonomic nervous systems utilizing Heart Rate Variability (HRV) technologies.

In a peer-reviewed paper published in *Neuroscience and Biobehavioral Reviews* in 2011, Julian F. Thayer and a team of experts on HRV describe it as, " … the sequence of time intervals between heartbeats. This inter-beat interval time series is used to calculate the variability in the timing of the heartbeat." They concluded, "Relative increases in sympathetic activity are associated with heart-rate increases and relative increases in parasympathetic activity are associated with heart-rate decreases." Thayer is quoted as saying, "HRV is important not so much for what it tells us about the state of the heart ..." but "for what it tells us about the state of the brain."

Another peer-reviewed paper, prepared by the Task Force of the European Society of Cardiology and the North American Society of Pacing Electrophysiology on Heart Rate Variability, and published in 1996, concluded, "HRV has considerable potential to assess the role of autonomic nervous-system fluctuation in normal healthy individuals … "

FIG. 7.8 | A HEALTHY BALANCE

The autonomic nervous system balances inputs to the brain from two opposing but inseparable subconcious streams.

FIG. 7.9 | A CALM BUILDING ON AN EXCITING STREET

The nine-square pattern is exemplified by this San Francisco home.

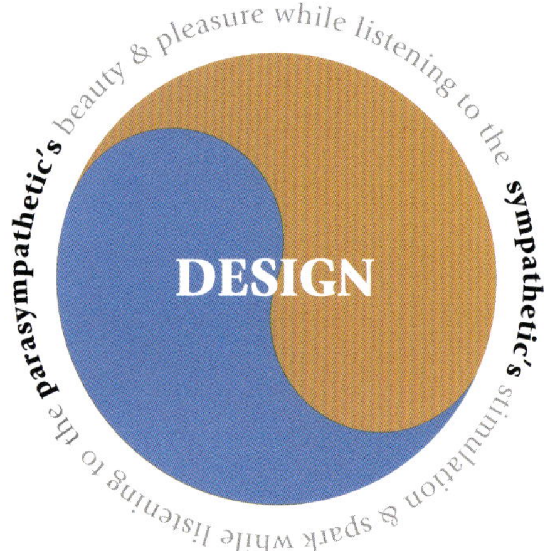

FIG. 7.10 | THE LEARNING CONTINUUM OF DESIGN

Design should work with an awareness of the autonomic nervous system's inputs.

A second tool, this one on the neuroscience front, is functional Magnetic Resonance Imaging (fMRI). This is the non-invasive brain imaging procedure that has "led researchers and physicians to be able to visualize the functioning of the brain for diagnostic treatment, and research purposes (***Essentials of the Brain*** 2013, R. Hatfield, Ph.D.).This cutting-edge technology has led to many remarkable discoveries and insights into the mysteries of the brain and is generally credited with revolutionizing the fields of neuroscience and medicine, and initiating the neuro revolution.

A third tool, which is in the architecture/computer category, is Virtual Reality (VR). This is described as a computer technology that uses headsets, sometimes in combination with physical spaces or multiprojected environments, to generate realistic images that simulate a user's physical presence in a virtual environment. Another form of VR is Augmented Reality (AR), which is a technology that superimposes a computer-generated image on a user's view of the real world, thus providing a composite view. Both of these newly developed technologies are becoming everyday tools used by the architectural profession to analyze design concepts. This is a development that portends new insights, methods and information to enrich art and architectural solutions.

Utilizing these tools, we now have the potential to compute the effects of the built environment prior to construction and to generate solutions that will help counter the epidemic of high-stress problems in society while simultaneously adding more pleasure and beauty to life. I believe this information can be culture-changing. If we continue to develop these technologies and combine them with advanced research in neuroscience and neuroaesthetics, then we can create a new model for design that heals ourselves and redirects the course that was initiated over a century ago.

For architecture and art, the conclusion is that we are on a slow and downward spiral with our current focus on stressful, adrenalized architecture and art. A better, healthier path forward would be to refocus on the utilization of recognizable, stress-relieving and calming patterns, with an emphasis on beauty for the betterment of all mankind. Concisely: Stress diminishes us. Beauty heals us.

Having developed new tools for visualization, measurement and quantification, science has opened an amazing window for architects and artists to improve society in profound ways. We have the opportunity to advance our information and knowledge into a plan of action that includes awareness and wisdom — awareness of current scientific thought combined with the wisdom of the past. It is an incredibly exciting and dynamic time for art and architecture brought on by advances in neuroscience.

FIG. 7.11 | RESISTANCE TO BEAUTY

Resistance to beauty neutralizes half of the inputs to the brain from the autonomic nervous system.

FIG. 7.12| ENDURING ARCHITECTURE

The Touro Synagogue, Newport, Rhode Island, 1763. It is the oldest synagogue building in North America. Architect: Peter Harrison

ONWARD AND UPWARD

"Beauty is free. Why wouldn't we use it?"

PIERO FERRUCCI, BEAUTY AND THE SOUL

I believe the time has come to try a different approach. I believe the past can release us from the tyranny of the present, that it can provide critical distance. I believe that the past can help us create a future in which scientific and technological innovation will support art's (and architecture's) enduring purpose — the enhancement of daily life.

ROBERT A.M. STERN

The significant problems we face today cannot be solved at the same level of thinking we were at when we created them.

ALBERT EINSTEIN

Progress lies not in enhancing what is, but in advancing toward what will be.

KAHLIL GIBRAN

Music is liquid architecture; architecture is frozen music.

JOHANN WOLFGANG VON GOETHE

Architecture and art are amazingly rich fields of thought. There is literally no end to the depth of learning available to those who seek out knowledge embedded there. They are connected to so many diverse human endeavors.

One of my areas of personal interest is music. I have played and studied classical piano for most of my life. Flowing from this base, I have long used musical analogies and metaphors to inform architectural concepts that we have developed at Ruggles Mabe Studio.

A good example is listening to one of the great symphonic works by Beethoven. Listening to Beethoven's Fifth Symphony is universally regarded as a beautiful and inspiring experience. The opening sequence is well-known and designed

THE AL-QARAWIYYIN MOSQUE. FEZ, MOROCCO

FIG. E.1 | BALANCED DESIGN

"Great architecture and art do not have to be just about parasympathetic forms."

The Milwaukee Art Museum Addition, Quadrucci Pavilion, designed by Santiago Calatrava, is an inspiring building. It combines very stimulating forms with elements of symmetry to create both pleasure and awe, stimulation and comfort.

Opposite: Inside the pavilion.

to gain your attention. It works! The opening movement has instances of power, excitement and awe, elevating our heart rates. The second movement includes passages of great calm and sonority, calming our heart rates, and the relaxation response takes over. Finally, the third movement returns to the more aggressive and spirited pace, and we are lifted up yet again.

Generally, the opening stanza is bold and catches your attention with a statement of the tonic cord. Then the piece moves off of the tonic with the development of the theme and subtle variations dancing around the tonic theme. Finally, with a flourish, the concluding variation is presented and includes the tonic theme. The overall sense at the conclusion is one of pleasure. Yet there have been brief moments of sympathetic cord structures and pace that set up extended passages of parasympathetic calm. The sympathetic anomaly is supported by the dominant parasympathetic fabric of the piece.

Today, in art and architecture, we are creating the sympathetic anomalies without the proper fabric to support the piece. The anomaly has become the norm. Everywhere we look, there are extreme flourishes with few supporting forms that speak to the parasympathetic nervous system.

Great architecture and art do not have to be just about parasympathetic forms. A sense of awe, beauty and wonderment can be achieved appealing to the sympathetic. The sympathetic event has an important place in our health and psyche, yet it needs to be supported by the parasympathetic as well. In fact,

homeostatic balance between sympathetic and parasympathetic responses is important to our well-being and a healthy nervous system. One should not be accentuated above the other.

We have heard and lived with the polemic that beauty isn't important to our lives for over a century now, much to our detriment. I recently read an interview in which a leading modernist architect was quoted as saying, "Ugliness is the next step in the pursuit of beauty." This attitude is being passed on in many universities most every day. I once attended a jury at an architectural school. During the presentation, one student used the word "beautiful" to describe an aspect of his presentation. The professor's reaction: "Don't ever use that word in this class again!" This is the attitude that we are living with. I firmly believe that no one set out to intentionally harm society. I simply believe that they did not have the information available to properly guide us. We do now.

In Chapter 6 we detailed how the push-pull between the two branches of the autonomic nervous system play out. It turns out that the sympathetic fight-or-flight reaction is five to seven times stronger than the parasympathetic. Nature prepares us first for survival, then asks questions later. Yet, this is a short-term reaction, and the relaxation response quickly restores us after the event has passed. Thus the parasympathetic effect and pleasure outlast the sympathetic.

The fight-or-flight reaction is an adrenalized one to a situation or pattern. Your nervous system is telling your body to remove itself from that situation due to danger and stress. Buildings and artwork that accentuate sympathetic qualities are essentially saying, "Go away. Stay away." Curiosity may draw us in, but once involved, the emotion is fight or flight. In the long term, these are the works we seek to avoid. Yet we continue to create adrenalized works because drama and uniqueness pique our curiosity. These qualities are short-lived. Concisely, we are creating and building societal stress that diminishes our lives.

As shown in Chapter 4, the buildings and artworks that utilize parasympathetic forms and create a sense of pleasure will be visited, honored and protected by society. These are places that you seek to revisit time after time. Timeless, iconic art and architecture are born of pleasure.

Architects have many responsibilities during a project. Each category is important and must be professionally managed. On the whole, as a profession, we are doing an exemplary job of caring for these issues. We are stopping short, though. Having solved the list of responsibilities too often means the work is finished. I believe that beauty and inspiration should be the overarching concepts. If we aren't creating something beautiful, then why do architects and artists exist? To create angst and stress? I'm not sure that is the role society is asking us to fulfill.

There is a spirited discussion going on in the architectural profession as well as the artistic community concerning traditional/classical styles versus contemporary modernism. It is a rhetorical stalemate. I believe the debate is centered on the incorrect set of concepts, though. We have new science available to elevate the conversation. The debate should be focused on what is the proper balance between sympathetic patterns and parasympathetic patterns, and how to enhance our well-being. The style discussion should develop from those concepts and not dictate them.

Beauty

Design
Site
Plan
Elevation
Section

Ethics
Sustainability
Client program
Context
Public good

Team Mangement
Construction timing
Contractor Relations
Subcontractor issues
Material availability
Utilization of tech

Fiduciary
Real estate values
Product development
International markets
Banking issues
Marketing

FIG. E.2
THE RESPONSIBILITIES
OF ARCHITECTURE

In the Preface, I wrote of a moment as a young man when I viewed a Frank Lloyd Wright drawing that changed my life. I reflected on how beauty and inspiration had propelled me through all of these years. And in the Introduction, I relived an encounter with a visitor to one of my projects early in my career who spontaneously proclaimed, "It's beautiful." Little did I know at the time the depth of that compliment or how profoundly important those words would become. It was inspirational and ignited a fire that continues to burn bright to this day.

Architects and artists can make a significant difference in changing our environment by utilizing natural and anthropomorphic patterns that generate parasympathetic reactions and avoiding patterns that create stressful, threatening sympathetic reactions. Two of the patterns that are known to create parasympathetic reactions are natural fractals and the nine square. There, no doubt, are many more to be identified.

Neuroscience, biology and psychology have provided architects and artists with the information and the means to improve our environment, and the health and well-being of society in general. As shown here, beauty enhances our health, our sense of well-being and our lives. The door is open to make a difference. Let's take the steps necessary to restore beauty to its rightful place of importance. We will all be the better for it.

FIG. E.3 | RESIDENCE DESIGNED BY RUGGLES MABE STUDIO

RESOURCES

Alexander, Christopher, *The Nature of Order, Book One*, Center for Environmental Structure, 2002

Alexander, Christopher, *A Timeless Way of Building*, Oxford University Press, 1979

Alexander et al, Christopher, *A Pattern Language*, Oxford University Press, 1977

Bachelard, Gaston, *The Poetics of Space*, Beacon Press, 1958

Barack, Lauren, "How Babies Learn About Feelings," *Parenting Magazine*

Beckley, Bill, *Uncontrollable Beauty*, Allworth Press, 1998

Biederman, Irving and Vessel, Edward, "Perceptual Pleasure and the Brain," *American Scientist*, 2006

Blackburn, Ph.D., Elizabeth and Epel, Ph.D., Elissa, *The Telomere Effect*, Grand Central Publishing, 2017

Boleyn-Fitzgerald, Miriam, *Pictures of the Mind*, Pearson Education/FT Press, 2010

Burke, Edmund, *A Philosophical Inquiry Into the Origin of Our Ideas of the Sublime and Beautiful*, Simon & Brown, 2013

Capra, Fritjof, *The Science of Leonardo*, Anchor Books, 2007

Changeux, Jean-Pierre, "Neuronal Man," Princeton University Press, 1985

Childre et al, Doc, *The Heartmath* Solution, Harper Collins, 1999

Churchland, Patricia S., *Braintrust*, Princeton University Press, 2011

Coburn, Alex; Vartanian, Oshin; and Chatterjee Anjan, "Buildings, Beauty, and the Brain: A Neuroscience of Architectural Experience," *Journal of Cognitive Neuroscience*, 2017

Costandi, Moheb, *Neuroplasticity*, MIT Press, 2016

THE LOUVRE PYRAMID
DESIGNED BY I.M. PEI

Curtis, N. Cortlandt, *The Secrets of Architectural Composition*, J.H. Jansen, 1923

de Botton, Alain, *The Architecture of Happiness*, Vintage/Random House, 2006

Doidge, M.D., Norman, *The Brain That Changes Itself*, Penguin Group, 2007

Eberhard, John P., *Brain Landscape*, Oxford University Press, 2009

Elam, Kimberly, *Geometry of Design*, Princeton Architectural Press, 2001

Goldberger et al, Ary, "Chaos and Fractals in Human Physiology," *Scientific American*, 1990

Goldberger, Dr. Al, "Fractals and the Birth of Gothic," *Molecular Psychiatry*, 1996

Habraken, N.J., *Palladio's Children*, Taylor & Francis, 2005

Huntley, H.E., *The Divine Proportion*, Dover Publications, 1970

Lehrer, John H., "Why Does Beauty Exist?", *Wired Magazine*, 2011

Lynch, Zack, *The Neuro Revolution*, St Martin's Press, 2009

Mallgrave, Harry Francis, *The Architecture of the Brain*, Wiley-Blackwell, 2011

Montgomery, Charles, *The Happy City*, Farrrar, Straus and Giroux, 2013

Morton, J. and Johnson, M., "CONSPEC and CONLERN: A Two-Process Theory of Infant Face Recognition," American Psychological Association, 1991

Nanda, Upali, *Sensthetics*, AkademikerVerlag, 2012

Norberg-Schultz, Christian, *Meaning in Western Architecture*, Praeger Publishers, 1975

Onderko, Patty, "The New Science of Mother-Baby Bonding," *Parenting Magazine*

Orians, Gordon H., *Snakes, Sunrises, and Shakespeare*, University of Chicago Press, 2014

Pallasmaa, Juhani, *The Eyes of the Skin*, John Wiley & Sons, 2012

Perez-Gomez, Alberto, *Attunement*, MIT Press, 2016

Pert, Ph.D., Candace, *Molecules of Emotion*, Scribner, 1997

Reisner (ed), Yael, *Architecture and Beauty*, Wiley & Sons, 2010

Perrett, David, *In Your Face*, Palgrave MacMillan, 2010

Robinson, Sarah and Pallasmaa, Juhani, *Mind in Architecture*, MIT Press, 2015

Rovelli, Carlo, *Seven Brief Lessons on Physics*, Riverhead Books, 2014

Rowe, Colin, *The Mathematics of the Ideal Villa and Other Essays*, MIT Press, 1976

Ruskin, John, *Seven Lamps of Architecture*, Ballantyne Press, 1849

Schinz, Alfred, *The Magic Square*, Edition Axel Menges, 1996

Schroeder, Gerald L., *The Science of God*, Free Press/Simon & Schuster, 1997

Schwarzer, Gudrun and Leder, Helmut, *The Development of Face Processing*, Hogrefe & Huber, 2003

Scruton, Roger, *The Aesthetics of Architecture*, Princeton University Press, 1979

Silver, John, *Architecture of the Absurd*, Quantuck Lane Press, 2007

Sternberg, M.D., Esther M., *Healing Spaces*, Harvard University Press, 2009

Thayer et al, Julian, "A Meta-Analysis of Heart Rate Variability and Neuroimaging Studies," *Neuroscience and Biobehavioral Reviews*, 2011

Thompson, D'Arcy, *On Growth and Form*, Cambridge University Press, 1961

Turati, Chiara; Simion, Francesca; Milani, Idanna; and Umilta, Carlo, "Newborns' Preference for Faces: What is Critical," *American Psychological Association Inc.*, 2002

Wexler, Bruce, *The Brain and Culture*, MIT Press, 2008

Zeisel, John, *Inquiry by Design*, W.W. Norton & Company, 2006

LANTERN AT HASEDERA TEMPLE, KANSAI, JAPAN

OPPOSITE: CLARK HALL, UNIVERSITY OF ALABAMA, TUSCALOOSA

CLARK HALL
ARTS AND SCIENCES

RESIDENCE BY
RUGGLES MABE
STUDIO

BIBLIOGRAPHY

Carter, Rita, *Mapping the Mind*, University of California Press, 1998

Chatterjee, Anjan, *The Aesthetic Brain*, Oxford University Press, 2013.

Churchland, Patricia S., *Braintrust*, Princeton University Press, 2011

Dissanayake, Ellen, *Art and Intimacy: How the Arts Began*, University of Washington Press, 2000

Dutton, Denis, *The Art Instinct: Beauty, Pleasure and Human Evolution*, Bloomsbury Press, 2008

Eberhard, John P., *Architecture and the Brain: A New Knowledge Base from Neuroscience*, Greenway Communications, 2007

Ferrucci, Piero, *Beauty and the Soul: The Extraordinary Power of Everyday Beauty to Heal Your Life*, Tarcher, 2009.

Gopnik, Allison; Meltzoff, Andrew N.; and Kuhl, Patricia, *The Scientist in the Crib: What Early Learning Tells Us About the Mind*, HarperCollins Publishers, 2000

Haidt, Jonathan, *The Happiness Hypothesis: Finding Modern Truth in Ancient Wisdom*, Basic Books, 2006

Hanlon, Don, *Compositions in Architecture*, John Wiley and Sons, 2009

Hatfield, Rudolph C., *Essentials of the Brain: An Introductory Guide*, Fall River Press, 2013

Kandel, Dr. Eric, R*eductionism in Art and Brain Science: Bridging the Two Cultures*, Columbia University Press, 2016

Kandel, Dr. Eric, *The Age of Insight: The Quest to Understand the Unconscious in Art, Mind, and Brain from Vienna 1900 to the Present*, Random House Publishing Group, 2012

Mallgrave, Harry Francis, *Architecture and Embodiment: The Implications of the New Sciences and Humanities for Design*, Routledge, 2013

Mandelbrot, Benoit, *The Fractal Geometry of Nature*, W.H. Freeman and Company, 1982

Marchant, Jo, *Cure, Mind Over Body*, Crown Publishing, 2016

Pinker, Steven, *The Blank Slate: The Modern Denial of Human Nature*, Penguin Books, 2003

Salingaros, Nikos A., *Unified Architectural Theory: Form, Language, Complexity*, Sustasis Foundation, 2012

Schinz, Alfred, *The Magic Square: Cities of Ancient China*, Axel Menges, 1996

Shermer, Michael, *The Believing Brain: How We Construct Beliefs and Reinforce Them as Truth*, Time Books, 2011

Sternberg, Ph.D., Esther, *Healing Spaces: The Science of Place and Well-Being*, Harvard University Press, 2010

Sussman, Ann; Hollander, Justin; *Designing for How We Respond to the Built Environment*, Routledge/Taylor & Francis Group, 2014

INDEX

NARA, HORYUJI TEMPLE, JAPAN

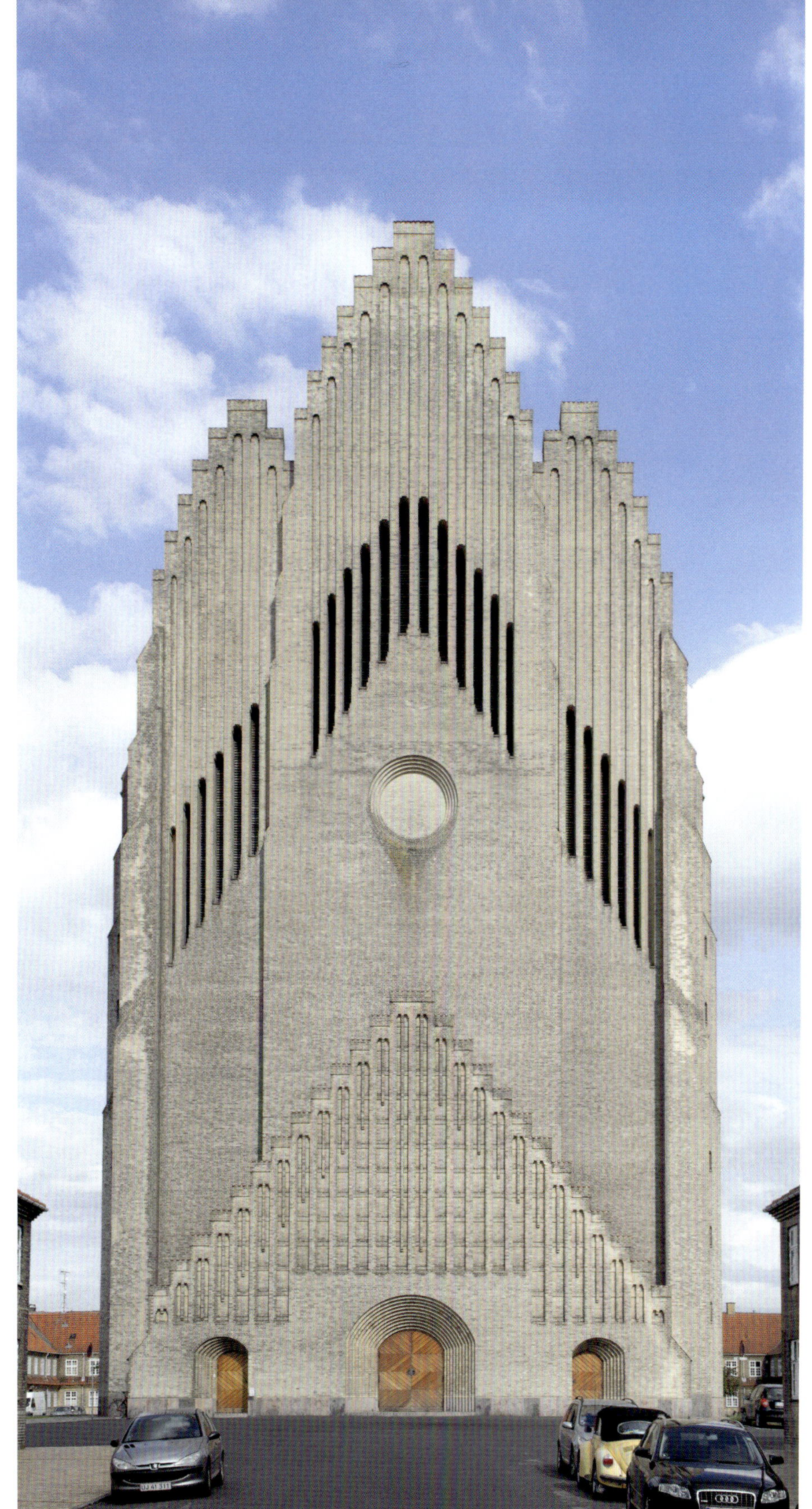

GRUNDTVIG CHURCH, COPENHAGEN
THE INTERIOR IS SHOWN ON PAGE 18

ON THE WEB

neuro-architectology.com

The Center for Beauty, Neuroscience & Architecture seeks to expand the boundaries of architectural and design thinking by providing innovative learning content for professionals, students and thought leaders.

IN FILM

built beautiful, an architecture & neuroscience love story

Directed by Mariel Rodriguez-McGill, produced by Barbara Bridges, and Donald Zuckerman, narration by Martha Stewart, 78 min. The film's main message: architects and designers have a responsibility to design with the well-being of humankind in mind.

COLOPHON

This book was designed by John Boak. He set the book in ITC Giovanni, a font designed by Robert Slimbach. The architectural plan and elevation drawings in the nine-square diagrams were created by Dakota Walters.

PHOTO CREDITS

Page vi, Linda Keller

Pages *x*, 32,102, Jim Scholz at Scholz Images

Page *xiv*, Mile High, Drawing #5617.002 | **Page 50**, Fallingwater Rendering. Drawing #3602.004. ©2017 Frank Lloyd Wright Foundation, Scottsdale, AZ. All rights reserved. The Frank Lloyd Wright Foundation Archives (The Museum of Modern Art | Avery Architectural & Fine Arts Library, Columbia University, New York)

Page 11, Steve Hall, Hedrich Blessing

Page 71, Bush Barrow Lozenge | Photo courtesy Dave Bukach / University of Birmingham. ©Wiltshire Museum, Devizes, UK

Page 80, Peter Vitale Photography

Page 110, David Marlow Studio

Page 114, Author photo: Paul Abdoo, Abdoo Studio

ABOUT THE AUTHOR

Donald H. Ruggles, AIA, NCARB, ICAA

Donald H. Ruggles not only has been a practicing architect for almost 50 years, he also has served with numerous boards and organizations to advance the profession. He is the president of Ruggles Mabe Studio, Architecture and Interior Design, founded in 1970 and based in Denver, Colorado. Ruggles was the founding president of the Institute of Classical Architecture & Art Rocky Mountain Chapter, serving for seven years.

In addition, Ruggles serves on the Board of Advisors for the University of Colorado Denver College of Architecture and Planning. He is on the board for the Human Architecture & Planning Institute in Concord, Massachusetts, and the Building Beautiful Institute in Sorrento, Italy. He has served as an awards juror for various local, regional and national organizations. He is a member of American Institute of Architects, National Council of Architectural Registration Boards, Institute of Classical Architecture & Art, and the Academy of Neuroscience for Architecture.